Contracting out

water and sanitation services

Contracting out

water and sanitation services

Volume 1

Guidance Notes for Service and Management Contracts in Developing Countries

*Kevin Sansom, Richard Franceys,
Cyrus Njiru & Javier Morales-Reyes*

Water, Engineering and Development Centre
Loughborough University
2003

WEDC

Water, Engineering and Development Centre
Loughborough University
Leicestershire
LE11 3TU UK

Cranfield
UNIVERSITY
Silsoe

Institute of Water and Environment
Cranfield University
Silsoe, Bedford
MK45 4DT UK

Produced as part of a WEDC/IWE partnership

Published by WEDC

ISBN 13 Paperback: 9780906055977
ISBN Library Ebook: 9781788532815
Book DOI: http://dx.doi.org/10.3362/9781788532815

A catalogue record for this book is available from the British Library.

Sansom, K. R., Franceys, R. W. A., Morales-Reyes, J. I. and Njiru, C. (2003) *Contracting Out Water and Sanitation Services – Volume 1: Guidance Notes for Service and Management Contracts in Developing Countries*

WEDC, Loughborough University, UK.

A reference copy of this publication is also available online at:
http://www.lboro.ac.uk/wedc/publications/cowss1.htm

This edition is reprinted and distributed by Practical Action Publishing.
Since 1974, Practical Action Publishing has published and disseminated books and information in
support of international development work throughout the world. Practical Action Publishing trades
only in support of its parent charity objectives and any profits are covenanted back to Practical Action
(Charity Reg. No. 247257, Group VAT Registration No. 880 9924 76).

This document is an output from a project funded by the UK
Department for International Development (DFID)
for the benefit of low-income countries.
The views expressed are not necessarily those of DFID.

Acknowledgements

The valuable assistance and contributions of engineers, managers and consultants from around the world has enabled the editors to assemble a diverse and interesting collection of contracting out case studies on the water sector in low- and middle-income countries, that have been included in Volume 2 of this publication. This material has enabled the authors to develop the Volume 1 Guidance Notes.

We would particularly like to thank the other co-authors of the case studies including Greg Weatherdon, Silver Mugisha, Vijay Gawade and Widi Hastuti. We also appreciate the assistance of the World Bank, the Water and Sanitation Program in Delhi and Nairobi, as well as Bernard Collignon and Mehra Metha. Their articles contributed to the development of case studies that enabled us to capture more of the diversity of the contracting out experiences in the water sector.

We would also like to extend our thanks to DFID for funding this work and to DFID's staff and Ian Curtis in particular, who have been supportive, despite delays and problems associated with data collection.

Numerous water utilities, government departments, municipalities and private operators around the world gave up valuable time in assisting with our field work and providing information, for which the editors are grateful.

List of boxes

List of figures

List of tables

Contents

Chapter 1

Introduction

The challenge of providing improved water and sanitation services, particularly in middle- and low-income countries (MLICs), is substantial. Private sector participation is increasingly seen as a key component of sector reform strategies aimed at improved service provision for all consumer groups. In recent years, there has been a trend of increased use of contracting out of water and sanitation services using service and management contracts. This has taken place in most parts of the world, including MLICs.

Where local conditions and the institutional environment are conducive, more complex Public Private Partnership (PPP) arrangements (such as BOTs, concessions and leases) potentially offer substantial benefits, perhaps because of the increased opportunity for delegating overall responsibility. There are many towns and cities in MLICs, however, where the local conditions are not yet suitable for such PPP arrangements, or where there may be a lack of willingness to implement these options, or where there may be limited private sector or regulatory capacity.

Contracting out through service and management contracts between a water service provider and a private contractor or operator, appear to be simpler to implement with the potential to deliver substantial benefits. This is particularly true when allied with good commercial practices by the utilities and the contractors, with a continuing understanding of the need for an effective partnership. The main PPP contract options are defined in section 3.1, which is entitled 'Key contract options.'

This document focuses on the use of service and management contracts. The key question addressed is:

'How can the use of contracting out be further enhanced to deliver improved water and sanitation service provision in developing countries?'

The first chapter broadly considers the wider view and lessons of contracting out and outsourcing in high- and middle-income countries. The remainder of this document focuses on how to improve service and management contracts for water and sanitation services in MLICs. Guidance is given on the development of contracting out strategies and appropriate contracts, including issues surrounding services for poorer communities. Chapters 4, 5 and 6 elaborate on the 22 guiding principles for contract development that emerged from the contracting out water services research programme. Examples of approaches and contract clauses that have been primarily used in MLICs are included. The example clauses and processes are intended to provide ideas for interested organizations to develop their own strategies and contracts that are appropriate for their specific local working environment. The aim is to encourage the development of balanced contracts with incentives to achieve win-win outcomes for all parties and thereby benefit the consumers.

Readers are referred to Volume 2 of this publication entitled 'Contracting out water and sanitation services—case studies and analysis of service and management contracts in developing countries' (edited by Sansom, Franceys, Morales-Reyes and Njiru, 2003). Volume 2 includes detailed case studies primarily from Latin America, Asia, Africa and the USA, as well as contract analyses and a wider literature review, all of which have informed the development of these guidance notes. For more detailed lessons on contracting out of services, it is recommended that readers refer to Volume 2 (the case studies document).

The intended target audience for these guidance notes includes managers, engineers, policymakers and support staff, who are considering contracting out water sector services, or who wish to explore ways of making improvements to current contracts. Where planners are interested in developing larger management contracts or more complex PPP options such as lease, BOT and concession contracts, it is recommended that they refer to the World Bank's 'Toolkits for Private Sector Participation in Water and Sanitation,' 1997. This World Bank document provides comprehensive information on the issues to be considered when developing complex PPP contracts.

The final chapter of the guidance notes briefly considers some of the key issues in establishing an effective enabling environment for contracting out, such as legislation and policies, commercial approaches and contractor development. Where these issues are adequately addressed, the prospects for successful contracting out are substantially enhanced.

It is hoped that increased use of contracting out with either local or international private operators will occur and will lead to service improvements for all consumer groups.

Chapter 2

An overview of contracting out and outsourcing

Contracting out and outsourcing are now very commonly used in industry and business in general. This section shares some of that experience in middle- and higher-income countries by quoting extensively from a limited selection of texts (Johnson, 1997; Oates, 1998; the Outsourcing Institute and *The Outsourcing Journal*) and from relevant websites.

2.1   Definitions: contracting out, contracting and outsourcing

The term 'contracting out' as used in this study is the use of external agents through short-term agreements to undertake activities that have traditionally been carried out internally by government departments or agencies. The emphasis here is on the introduction of contracting out into areas that have traditionally been carried out internally in the particular host organization. For example, servicing and maintenance of vehicles by private garages may well be a significant new change for some public agencies that have traditionally used their own workshops.

There is some confusion as to the extent to which outsourcing differs from straightforward contracting—as in a construction contract. 'At its most basic level, outsourcing is simply buying in components that a manufacturing company used to make itself. Outsourcing is simply the "make versus buy" decision that organizations have always had to make. What has changed is that the number and capability of external suppliers has exploded. They offer specialized solutions for every conceivable aspect of a company's operations. Additionally, technology has made it easier than ever to integrate the operations of separate companies into a cohesive whole.' (Johnson, 1997).

However, others would stress that the essence of contracting out is in the specification of the results that are expected to be achieved, rather than simply the output. In the publication 'Outsourcing …in brief', Johnson (1997) describes how 'it is important to separate what outsourcing really does into two distinct parts. Part one is a social and economic understanding, because it does bring with it disruption and rapid change to long-practised ways of work. Part two is what outsourcing means to organizations, how they implement it and what results they can expect from the process.'

The term outsourcing has also been used as a synonym for contracting out as shown by the Outsourcing Institutes' definition: '*Outsourcing is the strategic use of outside resources to perform activities traditionally handled by internal staff and resources.'* (Outsourcing Institute, 1998).

In this study, where the term outsourcing is used, the authors tend to follow the definitions above. However, Bendor-Samuel asks: 'Is "contracting" or "contracting out" just different terminology for "outsourcing?" These two terms are often confused, but they are not the same at all. Contracting is when a company (buyer) purchases goods or services from another company (supplier or vendor). In this situation, the buyer "owns" and controls the process. In other words, the buyer tells the supplier exactly what it wants and how it wants the supplier to perform those services. The supplier cannot vary from the buyer's instructions in any way. The buyer can replace the supplier quite easily by breaking the contract.'

'In outsourcing, the buyer turns over the control ("ownership") of the process to the supplier. The buyer tells the supplier what results it wants the supplier to achieve, but the supplier decides how to accomplish those results. In outsourcing, the supplier has expertise in a certain process (such as desktop computer systems, or human resources, or logistics etc.), and it has economies of scale. If the buyer were to dictate to the supplier how to do the job (as happens in contracting), the buyer would be destroying an important aspect that makes outsourcing work—the value that is created by using the supplier's expertise and economies of scale. Telling the supplier how to do the job also eliminates accountability on the part of the supplier, and this is an important element in successful outsourcing relationships.' Here is an example of printing services that are outsourced and that are contracted.

Contracted: The buyer says it wants 500 copies of the product. The buyer tells the supplier what kind and weight of paper to use, what method to use in binding the product (staple, glue, clips, brads etc.), how many people should be working on the project etc.'

'*Outsourced:* The buyer says it wants 500 copies of the product and they need to be first-rate quality, bound, produced at a cost that is lower than what it would cost the buyer to do in-house and accomplished faster than it could be done by the buyer in-house. Then the supplier decides how to accomplish the quality, lower cost, speed, what type of paper and binding to use etc.' (Bendor-Samuel, undated).

The authors acknowledge this distinction and look forward to the time when that level of sophistication and benefits could be achieved for water customers. For the purposes of this study, however, we recognize that the activities they have been investigating are closer to the 'contracting' end of the spectrum. The literature review that follows draws heavily on a limited (though representative) number of studies with a focus on 'outsourcing.' As outsourcing is the logical progression of the development of contracting out, the studies quoted provide a benchmark against which the water utility case studies (on contracting out in low- and middle-income countries) can be judged.

2.2 Guidance on outsourcing

David Oates in 'Outsourcing and the virtual organisation' (1998) gives one (of several) overviews of outsourcing in the high-income country commercial world. He stresses that the key for any organization is to keep the core activities and to outsource the non-core— *'sifting core from chore.'* However, the boundary between core and non-core seems to be moving over time as experience and confidence in outsourcing grows. Hence his subtitle: 'the incredible shrinking company,' as companies find they can move towards the virtual organization. 'Buying the best on the outside makes sense, as long as it leaves you to concentrate on the things you do best.' (Johnson, 1997). Water and sanitation utilities have to investigate what they do and then focus upon what they do best.

The underlying reasoning as to why companies grew and took responsibility for so many diverse activities in the first place is described in the following quote: 'More than 60 years ago Ronald Coase, a Nobel-prize-winning economist, explained why firms are vertically integrated (as opposed to individuals buying and selling goods and services at every stage of production). The main reasons, he said, were imperfect information and the need to minimize transaction costs. A firm can either produce component parts or services itself or buy them from a supplier. They will probably be cheaper if bought in the marketplace, but against that the firm will have to spend time and money on finding what is available, and on ordering the products.'

'In the past, these transaction costs were high, so firms often preferred to do lots of things in-house, which made them bigger. Vertical integration solved the problem of imperfect information. But as the Internet increases access to information and reduces transaction costs between firms and suppliers, it makes it more attractive for firms to concentrate on what they are best at and buy in other goods and services from outside. This reduces their optimal size. A small firm can now use accounting software rather than employing an accountant, a word processor instead of a typist, and email or voicemail instead of a telephone receptionist.' (The Economist, 2000).

For water and sanitation in middle- and low-income countries the authors are not particularly excited about the power of the Internet but recognize the need to balance the inherent inefficiencies of an integrated water company, particularly in terms of staffing, with the transaction costs of appointing private contractors in a transparent manner.

Oates (op. cit.) describes how deciding which activities are core or non-core is not as easy as it sounds. Catering and cleaning are clearly non-core, information technology can be seen to be a core activity but the mechanics of it are non-core. Accounting is non-core though financial management is core. Dealing with customer enquiries is being outsourced by many organizations whereas others see the relationship with the customer as being the heart of their business. 'The strategic issues for each firm will concern what is core and non-core. The operational issues will concern the process of managing the out-sourcing and the external contracts.'

'Core—the functions you perform for yourself when you have some real competitive advantage in the market.' (Oates, 1998).

'Organizations that aspire to be world-class in their own markets recognize they themselves cannot be world-class at everything. Yet only by gaining access to world-class services in all areas that are significant to their future business can they achieve the vital combination of quality and efficiency necessary for success' (PA Consulting in Johnson,

1997). 'The notion of "concentrating on what we do well" was widespread. Outsourcing "avoids training and career path issues with specialist staff."' (ibid).

Water companies have often had to develop specialist capacities that were not generally available in their economy at the time they were developed. In many cases these activities are now available, perhaps in the region if not in the country. Similarly, the dearth of adequate management capacity may well have justified an inclusive approach. With wider education and deregulation of many economies there is a much larger pool of private sector talent to draw upon. 'The key reason outsourcing is changing is that it isn't based simply on lower price, it is based on perceived quality and the type of fit an organization can make: does its culture integrate with your own or just grate?'

'Outsourcing isn't a new idea. The only thing that is new is that the imperatives have changed somewhat and are changing again right now.' (Johnson, 1997).

The kind of outsourcing agreement depends on the relationship with the contractor. At one end of the spectrum it is entirely transactional—the contractor gets paid for what is done. For example, to sweep four times a day and get paid for it. The client sets up monitoring to measure sweeping. At the other end of the spectrum, there is a relationship where it is agreed that the aim is to keep the end customer satisfied—'the partnership replaces clear specification linked to payment on delivery with some notion of relationship. That will involve issues concerning trust and openness and a willingness to be flexible about the terms of the contract provided the end result is perceived as satisfactory to the customers.' (Oates, 1998).

Clearly a contractor might prefer to bid to undertake an activity which is easier to price and reduces the transfer of risk; the customer, however, wants results which Oates describes as requiring partnerships. Partnership, 'acting together and deciding together' according to one definition, is a critical aspect of achieving the promised improvement in quality of outputs. The demand for partnership within any contracting out relationship is an important aspect of both the potential and the difficulty of replicating effective contracting out in different settings.

The need for partnerships based on trust and openness has to be balanced with the understanding that it is competition within the private sector that delivers. Contracting out demands that there is a possibility that the contractor, however strong the partnership, can be dismissed at the agreed notice in order for the client to change their pattern of outsourcing or to reduce costs.

There has to be a level of interdependence that is mutually beneficial. If you can both operate entirely separately and still deliver, you don't need a partnership, but if the contractor needs access to information or people inside the company, there is clearly a need for an approach that is close to a partnership.

As soon as the contract has to be at the partnership end of the spectrum in order to deliver the desired benefits, you run into the problems of asymmetry of information, more formally known as principal-agent theory. The principal (the client) cannot immediately know the calibre and the ongoing performance of the contractor. At all costs he wants to avoid 'buying a lemon.' But he may not know what he has bought until some way into the contract. As was described earlier in the quotation from Ronald Coase, imperfect information can lead to problems.

Very often a vertically integrated organization is not perfect, but the tasks are achieved at some level of quality. With contracting out, it is possible to optimize certain processes but it is also possible for the process to fail if the contractor fails.

Keeping activities in-house is insurance that you can always get the task done somehow. Contracting out is akin to gambling on the capabilities of others in the hope of optimizing an activity. The key for business, then, is in how to develop a competitive market for out-sourcing—a competition that delivers competent contractors who, more important than judging by price, can be measured on long-term quality.

In developed economies, the role of contracting out is seen in the potential for specialization. Here, the vertically integrated organization of the past is replaced by the networked organization of the future. As well as partnerships, innovation and alliances become key concepts. 'Innovation is the convergence of specialization and alliances—all taking place under the framework of an outsourcing agreement.' (Oates, 1998).

'What has emerged is that there are clearly two levels of approach to outsourcing. The first uses outsourcing as 'contracting out,' to achieve tactical benefits in the generally accepted way. The second approach appears to be founded on a fundamental reappraisal of the business model and modes of operation that a company uses. In this approach, external parties are brought in (rather than pieces of the business being disposed of) as part of a structural change in that business model.' (Johnson, 1997).

Therefore *strategic* sourcing (i.e. management contracts) rather than *tactical* outsourcing becomes the most effective way to optimise, but this is a real challenge to economies that have to operate tactically.

Returning, therefore, to the ideas of core competence, Johnson makes the pertinent comment that the ability to outsource well has to become one of the new core competences. 'The notion of outsourcing well (outsourcing professionally) is going to be a unique competence for many in the future, and one that will both define and assure their success. Outsourcing is being seen less and less as a tactical, cost-saving drive and more and more as a strategic direction that the organization follows.' (op. cit.). A management consultant (KPMG) offers the following guidance on best practice for outsourcing:

2.2.1   Best practice guidelines for outsourcing

The 'KPMG Impact Programme' offers the following guidelines:

Management issues
- Retain in-house control over strategic direction

- Retain responsibility for setting standards to which the supplier must conform

- Use a prime contractor

- Make the supplier responsible for delivery

- Be prescriptive about the service requirements rather than the method of service delivery

- Never lose sight of the business-driven objectives of outsourcing

- Avoid lock-in to any single supplier

- Expect value for money, but accept the supplier's need to make a profit—a partnership

- Understand the strategic, political and managerial implications of the scope of your outsourcing

- Define the supplier's point of contact—ensure adherence

- Have an appropriate person to manage the contract

- Keep the procedures simple

- Regularly review the outsourcing contract and relationship with the supplier

- NEVER stop negotiating

- Re-tender contracts at defined intervals

- Regularly review the outsourcing market to identify trends and changes

- Monitor the supplier's resource levels and business knowledge

- Encourage co-operative contract evolution and take advantage of developing technologies

- Retain and exercise the right to conduct audits at the supplier's premises

- Aim for continuous improvement

Human resources issues

- Ensure a sufficient number and quality of in-house staff remain to manage the outsourced situation

- Promote a continuing bond between supplier staff and end-users

- Sort out personality conflicts as soon as possible

- Regularly review in-house staff skills and numbers

- Involve end-users in monitoring service delivery against targets

- Retain the right to veto the supplier's choice of key staff

Service/business issues

- Match expectations with needs, not historical achievements

- Have a contingency escape plan covering the outsourcing contract

- Maintain the right to invite tenders for new work

- Recognize that requirements will change and be willing to adjust costs accordingly

- Ensure that service level agreements are always realistic and do not expect them to remain static

- Continue to benchmark the service and consider alternative approaches

- Discuss with all concerned, and at the earliest possible stage, plans which could affect services

Communications issues
- Clearly define the scope and interface of what is outsourced

- Establish unambiguous roles and responsibilities for the customer, end-user and supplier

- Maintain regular customer/supplier contact at various levels—even when things are going well

- Establish an open relationship, be prepared to compromise

- Build a relationship of trust with the supplier

- Hold regular meetings to monitor achievements

- Define clear escalation procedures

- Do not abuse escalation procedures—nit-picking with mangers is counter-productive

- Encourage the supplier to propose changes based on their expertise

- Ensure customer awareness, understanding and commitment

(KPMG, 1995).

2.3   Why contract out? The benefits

The first reason that is usually given for contracting out is to cut costs. Typically companies report a nine per cent reduction in operating costs in outsourced functions. However, Johnson (1997) reports a consequent '15 per cent improvement in capacity and quality. The least success is found in cases where financial savings have driven the transaction too hard.' Effectiveness as well as efficiency has to be an equal driver for contracted services.

In a *Study on Outsourcing*, Andersen Consulting (1993) found the motivation for outsourcing to be 'reduced costs, better value for money, improved quality of service, expertise, reduced management structure, increased flexibility.'

Another study reported that 'the main benefits of outsourcing are that it: frees management time, reduces staff costs, increases flexibility, improves cost certainty, reduces staff management problems and improves consistency of service.'

Oates (1998) adds to the list of reasons for contracting-out by suggesting that 'outsourcing objectives are normally rather simplistic single goals such as cost saving, but increasingly the decision to outsource is based on a desire to bypass internal politics. In one example, the client wanted a system of standardization in its financial activities across all its businesses with economies of scale. By ripping it out of the organization and handing it over to external experts all the hassle of internal wrangling over who would be responsible

---

Box 2.1. Top 10 reasons why companies outsource[1]

- To reduce and control operating costs
- To improve company focus
- To gain access to world-class capabilities
- To free internal resources for other purposes
- Because resources are not available internally
- To accelerate re-engineering benefits
- Because a function is difficult to manage/out of control
- To make capital funds available
- To share risks
- To facilitate a cash infusion

---

1.   Source: Survey of Current and Potential Outsourcing End-Users, The Outsourcing Institute Membership, 1998

for what and what policies would be adopted were dealt with at a single stroke.' He goes on to explain how this was not the declared objective 'but in practice it was the rationale behind the decision.'

Clearly this is also one of the reasons behind large scale Public Private Partnerships in MLIC water utilities. One of the questions this study has to try to answer is the extent to which this desire to influence institutional development can be delivered by contracting out in less sophisticated management environments.

The literature emphasizes that it is wrong to outsource a problem, 'abdication is not a solution, it is asking for trouble. The fact that someone can save you ten per cent does not mean the operation is efficient, it just means it is cheaper.' (ibid.).

It is also clear that effective outsourcing requires skilled management within the client organization if it is to make best use of the outsourced contract. It may well be that the internal management capability to contract out successfully is harder to acquire than any in-house performance of the task in the first place. Oates describes how disparate outsourced contracts required far more management resources than they were worth.

'Based upon a comprehensive survey of 95 industrial sectors in the UK during early 80s to early 90s, industrial sectors that were most profitable experienced the highest growth in outsourcing. This shows that outsourcing was not a response to failure but a strategy of success.' (ibid.).

A clear message, therefore, is that an enterprise will get the most benefits from contracting out where it is already well managed and competent at performing the particular task. 'Don't outsource a problem: outsource a solution—something that is running as efficiently as you can get it… Practically all outsourcing experts agree that companies planning to hand over operations to a third party should first get their own house in order. Companies should not outsource because they want to get rid of a problem that they haven't taken the time and trouble to sort out for themselves. They should hand over a well-run operation, whatever function it is performing, to a third-party provider that can do an even better job.' (ibid.).

Oates goes on to emphasize that an enterprise should not necessarily outsource 'because you can't do it—but because there is a partner that can help you to be the best in the market.'

This ideal of optimization may not always be the imperative for some water utilities where a 'good enough' solution could well deliver a significant improvement to consumers.

2.4   The mechanics of contracting out

Johnson (1997) explains that one of the problems of contracting out/outsourcing is that 'no one seems quite sure what it really is and the extent of the activities it covers.' According to research by The PA Consulting Group, the average number of functions outsourced by organizations has risen 225 per cent (from 1.2 to 3.9) over the past five years and will go on growing. The most frequent activities are quoted as: property services, catering and information technology '… but now there is clear evidence that outsourcing is moving from peripheral activities towards more central ones.'

The Outsourcing Institute (1998) describes three phases of outsourcing:

*   Internal analysis and evaluation

*   Needs assessment and vendor selection

*   Implementation and management

'In Phase 1, senior management examines the need for outsourcing and develops a strategy to implement it. This phase is mostly internal and conducted in the highest level of the organization. For an organization to benefit from outsourcing, the initiative should come from the top. Only the top-level executives have the power to define the vision and implement the changes that are necessary for outsourcing to succeed. As you develop a strategy, consider the following:

*   Clarify organizational goals in relation to outsourcing.

*   Identify areas to outsource. Define the core competencies of the organization and the functions of the business that are not core. An organization should outsource its non-core functions so that it can focus on its core competencies. Having identified non-core functions, gather facts and figures to determine where you will get the quickest and best return on investment. To determine the return on investment, analyze current return compared to what an outside vendor may offer.

*   Develop a long-term strategy. If you are outsourcing a function that already exists, remember that employee support and morale will be critical. Job retention should be a major feature of your strategy. In some relationships, workers are hired by the new vendor or operator. From the beginning, communicate honestly and openly with employees about how their needs will be met.

'In Phase 2, people inside and outside of the organization provide more detailed information and advice. This is a research phase in which you learn about your own specific needs, and find out which qualified vendors will be best to meet those needs. To find out more about your own needs, research the needs within the organization, and learn from other companies who have outsourced the same kind of function. Plan to visit these companies to find out what their experience has been. Form a team of people to help you ask the right questions and analyze the information you gather. You may need team members with expertize in the following areas:

- legal

- human resources

- finance

- procurement

- the specific function to be outsourced.

'By now you have learned quite a lot about specific services, costs and other issues pertaining to the function you wish to outsource. You will now write a request for proposal (RFP). A request for proposal should:

- be structured in a way that will allow assessments and comparisons to be done in meaningful way;

- define requirements in complete and measurable terms;

- describe the type of relationship you are looking for;

- explain the problems that you are trying to solve;

- ask specific questions about corporate culture;

- present the current costs to the organization; and

- specify a service level.

'It is best to be honest. A proposal is a valuable opportunity for a vendor to grapple with very real costs and problems and prove to you that they can do an excellent job. Just as you will use the proposals to assess vendors, vendors use your RFP to assess you. A well-written, clearly defined RFP tells vendors you are serious about the project. They will work hard to solve your problems and get your business. On the other hand, a vague or unrealistic RFP will make the most qualified and experienced vendor think twice before spending any time going after business that may be unprofitable and unmanageable.

Form a team to review proposals. The team should identify which vendor comes closest to meeting your needs. As they assess proposals, team members should use networks and references to find out about a vendor's reputation in the industry and look at the vendor's total plan and capabilities, not just price or a single aspect of what they do. To make the right choice, be sure the vendor demonstrates:

- a clear understanding of your needs and an ability to solve your problems;

- financial stability;

- cultural fit; and

- a proven track record.

Once the vendor has been chosen, you will negotiate and sign a contract. In this you should:

Box 2.2. Top 10 factors in vendor/operator selection[1]

- Commitment to quality
- Price
- References/reputation
- Flexible contract terms
- Scope of resources
- Additional value-added capability
- Cultural match
- Existing relationship
- Location
- Financial stability and solvency

---

1. Source: Survey of Current and Potential Outsourcing End-Users, The Outsourcing Institute Membership, 1998. The latest findings from the Outsourcing Index.

- negotiate a reasonable price and performance measures;

- communicate often and openly;

- show your willingness for both sides to succeed; and

- write a contract that defines the service level and the consequences if the level is not met.

Decide in advance how you are going to manage the relationship. Create a system that allows you to:

- monitor and evaluate performance;

- identify and communicate issues early;

- resolve issues quickly and fairly; and

- help people in your organization adapt to a new way of doing things.

(The Outsourcing Institute, 1998).

Pragmatically, it is suggested that 'by far the best way of outsourcing is to divide and conquer, because by appointing a number of suppliers, a user can play them off against one another for the best deal.' Oates, however, goes on to explain that 'having made the deal, the emphasis should be on partnering: there should be "no ringing up and shouting down the phone if things go wrong." Rather "we are going to talk to them about why they are scoring low and what we as the customer can do to help them as the supplier to do a better job." The buyers who used to be told "Go out, and kick your suppliers" are now being told: "Be good to them and work together with them." It's a whole new world.' Oates (1998).

Oates describes the SESPA model of choosing contractors. SESPA stands for: 'supplier evaluation, selection and performance appraisal.' The 'SES' part is 'picking the winner' and the 'PA' part is 'measuring the winner's performance over the years against the same attributes with which they won the business.' The approach is that the company be totally

---

Box 2.3. Top 10 factors for successful outsourcing[1]

- Understanding company goals and objectives
- A strategic vision and plan
- Selecting the right vendor
- Ongoing management of the relationships
- A properly structured contract
- Open communication with affected individual/groups
- Senior executive support and involvement
- Careful attention to personnel issues
- Near term financial justification
- Use of outside expertize

---

1. Source: Survey of Current and Potential Outsourcing End-Users, The Outsourcing Institute Membership, 1998. The latest findings from the Outsourcing Index.

open with potential suppliers as to the characteristics against which they will be judged, and then it should give rigorous weighting to the attributes declared in the proposals from suppliers. For example, one company used thirty competences or attributes under SESPA to judge bidders for a contract to manage the company's global travel. 'We have not yet once had to sack a supplier we've picked through SESPA.'

Cross-functional teams are used to determine the criteria deemed important for any supplier. For example, 'responsiveness, market knowledge, communications, use of technology, competence in appropriate fields, approach to training, control of operations, approach to safety' were chosen as appropriate attributes for a contract to provide legal services. Significantly, it is reported that the SESPA process did not consider price as key factor in the evaluation. 'In fact only four out of 32 (in one example) competencies identified refer to price. This ensures that the decision is based on our total needs.' (ibid.).

Oates describes that 'it is not just what is being outsourced that is slowly changing, also the way in which it is being conducted ... some pioneers are trying out variations such as co-sourcing. While traditional outsourcing may be perfectly suitable for low-risk peripheral activities such as cleaning or car fleet management, with higher-risk strategic functions or processes, companies want to retain more say in the way in which the work is done. With co-sourcing, the client company keeps responsibility for the management and strategic aspects of the outsourced activity, while the outside provider supplies consultancy services and often experienced personnel to help the business streamline the function or process.'

It is clear that the progression through contracting out to outsourcing to relational contracting is continuing: 'after a decade of outsourcing in logistics, many of the 300 companies polled made it clear that they wanted more from the relationship that they were getting. They are looking to providers to offer a much more strategic and innovative input in the development of their distribution operations.' (ibid.).

2.5   Pricing contracting out transactions

The Outsourcing Journal gives a summary of the various approaches to structuring the pricing of an outsourcing contract.

- Cost plus. This approach pays the supplier for its actual costs, plus a predetermined percentage as profit. This plan allows little or no flexibility when business objectives and technology change during the life of the contract, nor does it give any incentive for the supplier to perform more effectively.

- Unit pricing. This is a set rate determined by the supplier for a particular level of service, and the client pays based on its usage. Paying for desktop maintenance based on the number of users is an example of this approach.

- Fixed price. Some buyers think this is the best approach, because they know exactly what the supplier's price will be, even in the future. Problems with this approach arise if the buyer does not adequately define the scope of the process and design effective standards before signing the contract. Too often the result in this case will be that the supplier claims that a particular service or service level is beyond the scope of the contract and then charges a premium for it.

- Variable pricing. This plan involves use of a fixed price at the low end of the supplier's service, with variances based on higher service levels. Its effectiveness, again, depends on adequately defining the scope of the work and the processes.

- Incentive-based (or performance-based) pricing. Here, the buyer provides incentives to encourage the supplier to perform at peak level (or to complete a one-time project ahead of time, for example) by offering a bonus reward if the supplier performs well. This plan works in the same way by ensuring that the supplier must pay a penalty if it does not perform to at least the 'satisfactory' service level designated in the agreement. This plan is the one to use to ensure the supplier's excellence in performance.

- Risk/reward sharing. Here, the buyer and supplier each have an amount of money at risk and each stand to gain a percentage of the profits if the supplier's performance is optimum and achieves the buyer's objectives.

- The buyer will select a supplier using a pricing model that best fits the business objectives the buyer is trying to accomplish by outsourcing (<outsourcing-journal.com>, 2001).

2.6   Lengths of contracting out and outsourcing contracts

Emphasizing the partnership aspects of contracting out, Oates describes how 'the best outsourcing deals have no expiry date—they are "evergreen." Naturally both parties have to have an escape clause, but it is recommended that this should not be the normal thirty days but rather around six months, so that the contractor has the confidence to innovate and invest in doing things better. Having 'no expiry date' does not mean signing long-term contracts (10 years, for example) that lock you into a supplier. It is not good for a company to be bound to a contractor that might be waning as other suppliers grow in effectiveness and efficiency. 'Most of them think five years is about right' to get benefits of partnering but not lose the benefits of competition.

'So the length of a deal is primarily the amount of investment you expect the supplier to make. Some of that will be efficiency type investment, but some of it may be relationship-building investment. If you are building a capability type service, that only begins to deliver after two or three years, it would be stupid to cut it off at that point.'

Figure 2.1 illustrates one aspect of the apparent contradiction between competition and partnership. Competition delivers the price and quality aims at the bidding stage, the effects of which decline the longer the contract continues. Partnering, where the client and contractor seek to work together actively to mutual advantage, needs a longer-term contract to achieve benefits beyond those which a client might achieve by appointing the lowest bidder. The challenge for any service or management contract is how to combine these two benefits.

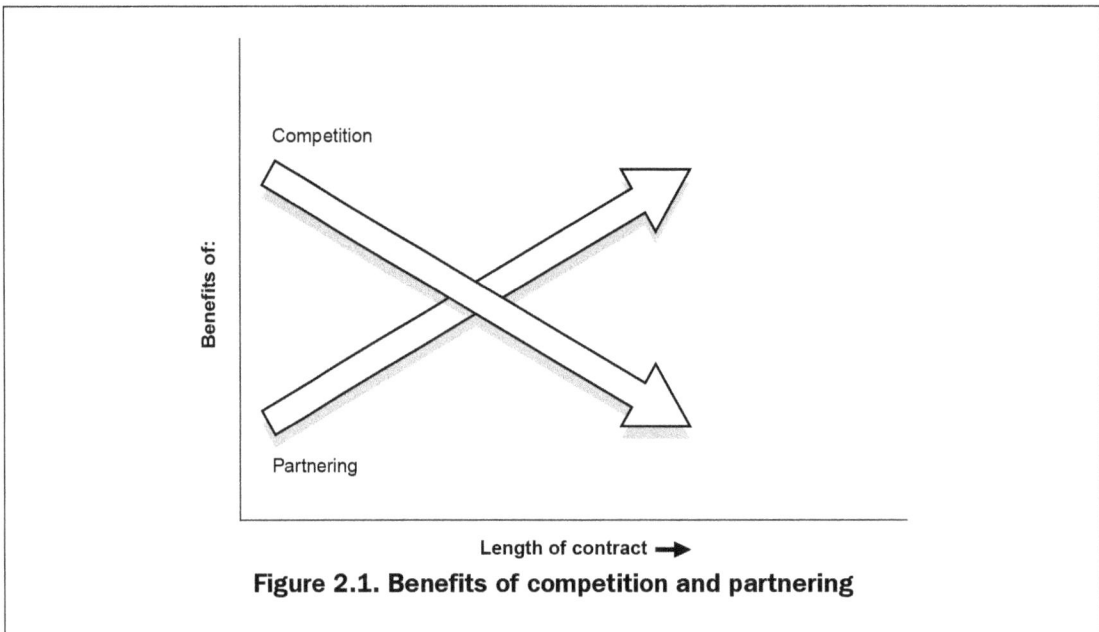

Figure 2.1. Benefits of competition and partnering

Some researchers have found that 'there is a remarkable tendency for companies to start to chafe at their outsourcing relationships at about the second year; this is often when contract adjustments are needed. This "two-year itch" phenomenon is another reason why a three-year contract makes sense. An adjustment process can take three to six months and, if the supplier isn't willing to work with the buyer, they're not far from being able to go out to market. That implied threat of going out to the market puts the buyer in a strong position to make sure that there will be fair and equitable negotiations.'

The best way that the authors have found to achieve flexibility is with a long-term master contract for a relationship that could last ten years (which is in the supplier's interest), with adjustments to the shorter-term service agreements underneath it as necessary (which is in the buyer's interest), and with added incentives along the line (which is in both parties' interests) (Outsourcing Journal, 2001).

2.7   Monitoring the contract

Much advice is given as to the monitoring of contracts. The best way to sum up the approach to monitoring is in the quote: 'outsourcing is similar to delegation, you can outsource but you can't walk away.' (Oates, 1998).

To maintain effectiveness, you must have good reporting systems and a tight control on costs. However, maintaining the partnership approach, arrangements should be seen as 'service level agreements' rather than contracts. Company's should also recognize that if the partnership is to deliver and remain alive, the agreement and the underlying document may well have to be reviewed at least every six months. 'I think the real measure of success is that the service level agreement, and the service management process we have around it, is dusted off and looked at a lot. But if the actual contract on which the service level agreement is based has to come out of the drawer, we have failed.' (ibid.).

The point is made that there is a shift in expectations with outsourcing. 'If it is internal, the in-house users expect a fall off in quality over time and expect to start doing things themselves to get round problems. If it is outsourced, it is more likely that expectations will rise, quite possibly beyond what the contract or agreement specifies.'

'The hard nosed would say that the best way to keep providers up to scratch is to keep them on short-term contracts, constantly aware that under-performance will mean the chop. This flies in the face of more modern supply chain management advocates, however, who would argue that by involving suppliers or sub-contractors closely and building up a relationship of trust, everyone can win.' (Oates, 1998).

Rehfuss (1993) lists the elements of a good monitoring system.

- Require that the contractor present periodic reports.

- Review those reports carefully for adherence to the written contract.

- Compare wage rates and equipment charges for materials or rentals with the contract.

- Verify that all services, material, labour and equipment were actually received, used or consumed.

- Initiate all change orders that affect the contract.

- Whenever possible, make on-site inspections. Report the results of those inspections, comparing accomplishment to the prescribed specifications.

- Follow up on every complaint.

- Survey citizen or user satisfaction whenever possible.

Not every contract can be a 'win.' The Outsourcing Institute (1998) report that 'Outsourcing relationships fail for many reasons. Chief among them are unrealistic expectations; lack of a formal bid process; so-called relational contracts that assume the vendor will act as a strategic partner, but that fail to spell out the details; and failing to manage the relationships once the contract has been signed.'

In conclusion, both the considerable benefits and the challenges faced by using contracting out and outsourcing are summarized in the following quotes from an Economist article.

- 'The main reason for contracting out is functional specialization. Thanks to contracting out, firms can combine the virtues of size (economies of scale, large pools of talent) with the benefits of trimness (focus, responsiveness and, above all, low overheads).

- 'Managers should remember that contracting out has two huge benefits: competition and transparency. Even if a job stays in-house, the threat of competition forces employees to cut their costs, curb their inclination to strike and, in a surprising number of cases, come up with innovative ideas. It also throws up invaluable information about relative costs.

- 'Though it looks simple, contracting out is remarkably hard to do well'

'Farming out the farm', The Economist, 1994.

Chapter 3

Contracting out strategies for the water sector

As the pressure increases for water utilities to provide a cost-effective, quality service to customers in a sustainable manner, the need to ensure sound management and value for money has led many utilities to contract out various services to the private sector. When a water utility contracts out services, the role of that utility can change from that of a direct service provider and manager of human resources to that of a service planner — defining the work to be delivered by the contractor, and letting and managing the contract.

Contracting out can be an important part of a utility/municipality's overall service improvement programme. It is, therefore, worthwhile for them to be systematic and comprehensive in developing appropriate strategies. Section 3 considers key contract options and potential strategies to be explored.

3.1 Key contract options

Selection of the appropriate type of contract for the provision of water and sanitation services needs to be carefully thought out and based on good information. Public Private Partnership contracts for water sector service provision have been conveniently categorized into a number of different types of contracts or PPP options. Table 3.1 gives a brief summary of the allocation of responsibilities between the private and public sector for each of the main types of contracts. It is clear that for service and management contracts many of the key responsibilities, apart from the specific functions that are contracted out, remain with the public sector.

The main types of service and management contracts in general use are briefly described in Box 3.1. Specific contracts can also be developed with features from two or more of these options. In general, these contracts do not include substantial investment funding, although in some cases loans or donor funding are allied to such a contract as part of a programme of general improvement.

Another form of management contract is the community/co-operative contract (refer to Box 3.2), which is becoming more common, particularly in informal settlements. Four case studies of these types of contracts are included in Volume 2 *Case studies and analysis of service and management contracts*, edited by Sansom et al (2003). Where utilities are considering how to improve services to informal settlements or compound areas, the authors recommend that they explore this form of contract or collaboration with

Table 3.1. Typical allocation of responsibilities between the public and private sector for the main contract types

Contract type	Asset ownership	Operation and maintenance	Capital investment	Commercial risk	Typical duration	Location of example contracts
Service contacts	Public	Public and private	Public	Public	1 to 3 years	Mexico City, Chile and Chennai, India
Management contracts	Public	Private	Public	Public	3 to 5 years	Trinidad and Tobago, Columbia, Uganda
Lease contracts	Public	Private	Public	Shared	8 to 10 years	Guinea, Cote d'Ivoire, Czech Republic
Concession	Public	Private	Private	Private	25 to 30 years	Buenos Aires, Argentina and Manila, the Philippines
BOT	Private and public	Private	Private	Private	15 to 25 years	Malaysia, Mexico
Divestiture	Private or private and public	Private	Private	Private	Not applicable	England and Wales

community groups. Further discussion of these types of arrangement is included in section 2.5.

The other broad category is the 'complex contracts' such as lease, BOTs and concessions, which are briefly described in Box 3.3. These contract options tend to be of a longer duration and require more preparation time and transaction costs, but can lead to substantial benefits in the right environment.

Figure 3.1 'Basic modes of water sector organization,' shows the continuum of increasing private sector management and increasing ownership of the utility, for the different types of contracts. For more information on the requirements and potential benefits of the different types of contracts, readers are referred to the *Toolkits for Private Participation in Water and Sanitation* The World Bank, Washington DC, 1997.

3.2   Developing strategies

3.2.1   Problem and objective analysis

First, it is necessary to consider what water sector functions could potentially be contracted out. Figure 3.2 shows the typical main functions that are necessary for the supply of urban water and sewerage services. These functions have been divided into 3 cores:

Box 3.1. Definitions of service and management contracts in the water sector

Service contracts are the simplest form of PSP whereby the public authority retains overall responsibility for services such as: operation and maintenance (O&M) of the system, except for the specific system components that are contracted out. The contractor's responsibility is limited to managing its own personnel and services efficiently. Typically, service contracts are used for maintenance of components such as pumping stations and meter reading. Payment is usually on a lump sum basis dependent on the contractor achieving certain agreed targets. In recent years incentive and penalty clauses have also been introduced. Typical contract duration is one to three years. Countries with these types of contracts include Chile, Mexico, India and Kenya.

A variation on the service contract is the *'labour only' contract* where the contractor essentially provides a specified number of staff for a specific purpose to a public authority, which maintains overall responsibility for providing the service. The public authority usually specifies the precise numbers and skill profile of the contract staff. The contractor is in effect acting as a contract staff agency. Under such a contract it is difficult to set performance standards, because the public authority makes the management decisions. It is generally only possible to replace unsatisfactory staff. This type of arrangement has been used in the Indian water sector.

Management contracts are more comprehensive arrangements where the public authority transfers responsibility to a private contractor for the management of a range of activities, such as the O&M of a water supply distribution system or major sub-system. Remuneration is usually based on a tendered fee. Those contracts that also have an incentive-based component, using parameters such as volume of water produced and improvements in bill collection rates, are generally more successful. The public authority usually finances working and investment capital and determines cost recovery policies.

Management contracts are often seen as a useful first step towards more complex PPP arrangements such as leases or concessions. Typical contract duration is from three to five years and occasionally up to 15 years. Countries with these types of contracts include: Uganda, South Africa, Mexico, Kenya and India. Two common forms of organizational arrangements for management contracts are as follows:

Joint public/private company. A new company is established for the purposes of the operation of the contract with staff and resources provided from both the government/utility and the private operator. This encourages shared ownership and hopefully shared benefits. This type of contract is generally used for a large-scale management contract, e.g. the management contract in Trinidad and Tobago.

Delegated management to a private operator entails the public authority handing over the responsibility for management of a full range of activities, such as O&M of a distribution system and/or billing and collection, to a private operator, e.g. Tongaat, South Africa and Malindi in Kenya.

- *Core 1* contains those regulatory functions that should not generally be contracting out, because they are the core responsibilities of the government/regulator.

- *Core 2* includes the main management functions.

- *Core 3* includes service, consultancy and construction functions that are more easily contracted out.

Box 3.2. Community/co-operative management contracts

Community/co-operative management contracts are contracts in which a community or user group manages some aspect of water or sanitation service provision in collaboration with a utility. For example, in an urban environment the community group may manage part of the tertiary water distribution water network and cost recovery from consumers in a defined area, while at the same time paying the utility for the bulk supply of water. There may or may not be a written contract and in some cases the community group may take over the management of assets. Countries with these types of contracts include Haiti, Kenya, Uganda and India.

Box 3.3. Definitions of 'complex contracts'

Lease contracts, also known as *Affermage*, are used where a private operator or lessor rents the facilities from a public authority and is responsible for operating and maintaining a complete system and collecting the tariffs. The lessor effectively buys the rights to the income stream from the utility's operations and thus assumes a significant share of the commercial risk associated with those operations. The lessor generally provides the working capital while the public authority provides the capital investment. The duration of a lease contract can be from five to 15 years. Countries with these types of contracts include France, Guinea, Poland and Senegal.

BOT (Build, Operate and Transfer) **contracts** are a form of concession whereby a private firm or consortium agrees to finance, construct, operate and maintain a facility for a specific period before transferring the fully operational facility (at no cost) to a government or other public body. BOT arrangements are attractive for new plants that require large amounts of finance, for example, large water treatment plants, but they are not commonly used for water distribution or wastewater collection systems. The contract period is normally greater than 20 years, sufficient for the private contractor to pay off loans and achieve a return on investment. These contracts often require relatively high tariffs and/or subsidies to meet the BOT operators' costs. Countries with these types of contracts include Brazil, Malaysia, Mexico and China.

Concession contracts are very substantial in scope—the private sector company takes on full responsibility not only for the O&M of the utility's assets, but also for investments, often for a whole city. Asset ownership remains with the government. Frequently the concessions are bid according to price—the bidder who proposes the lowest tariff to operate the utility and meet the specific investment and performance targets, wins the concession. The contract, which is usually over a period of 25 to 30 years, sets out the main performance targets, the mechanism by which prices can be adjusted over time and arrangements for arbitration of disputes between the project partners. Concessions generally require tariffs to be at a sufficiently high level at the start of the contract to meet the full costs of service provision. Countries with these types of contracts include: Argentina, Philippines, France and Malaysia.

The water utility could potentially use service contracts for each of the individual functions that are identified in core 3, while a management contract for the O&M of water supply, for example, would cover those functions that are underlined in cores 2 and 3. A concession contract, however, could be used for all the functions in cores 2 and 3, except for the ownership of assets. Hence, much more extensive preparations are required for such contracts.

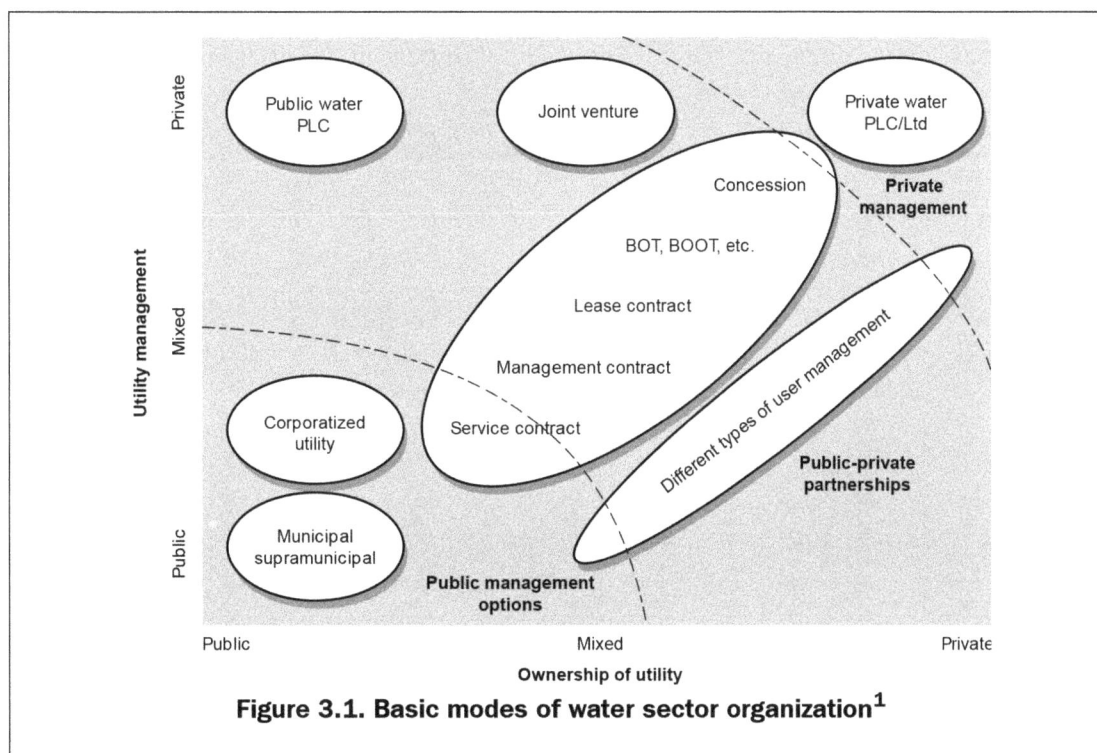

Figure 3.1. Basic modes of water sector organization[1]

1. Source: Blokland *et al.*(1999)

The 'ideal' and 'realistic' decision trees in Figure 3.1 and Figure 3.2 aid decision making when the public utility is determining whether to contract out a particular activity or not, and which problems to solve.

The key starting point is to understand the range and nature of tasks currently undertaken by the utility in terms of business processes, in conjunction with an accurate understanding of the costs and benefits linked to each process. Note that the 'realistic decision tree' includes more activities related to gaining support for contracting out.

When selecting which type of contract (service, management, lease etc.) to use utilities should be aware of the potential benefits of contracting out in the water sector. Many of the potential objectives for contracting out water and sanitation services are listed below.

1. To improve quality of service provision in terms of adequacy and reliability.

2. To make more effective use of existing infrastructure.

3. To introduce technical expertise (including technological advances/new technologies) to the sector.

4. To introduce improved commercial management.

5. To improve operating efficiency and system performance.

6. To introduce net savings in the costs of service provision and reduce subsidies.

7. To reduce political interventions in utility operations.

8. To introduce competition in the sector and act as a catalyst for change to the wider public water sector.

Core 3: Service functions

Core 2: Management functions

Core 1:
Customer protection and regulation of:-

- tafiffs, prices and value for money
- responsiveness to consumers
- service standards
- asset serviceability and efficiency
- safety net for poor
- water availability and use
- environmental and health standards
- infrastructure development for future needs
- performance related incentives

Core 2 items:
- □ management of billing and collection
- □ customer service system
- □ tariff revision proposals

- □ budgeting and accounting
- □ financial management
- □ internal audits
- □ financing working capital
- □ arranging capital finance

Management of O & M for water distribution

Management of O & M for bulk supply

Management of emergency water supplies

Management of water quality control

Management of wastewater treatment

Management of O & M of wastewater sewerage system

Major capital works development programme

Minor capital works development programme

Contract management

Ownership of assets

Utility property management and procurement

Vehicle management and procurement

Personnel and human resource development

Organizational restructuring

Core 3 items:
- Design implementation of a computer billing system
- Customer surveys

- Design implementation of a computer billing system
- External audits

Water demand assessment

Feasibility studies for future investment options and plans

Financing investment capital

New infrastructure feasibility studies

Capital works designs

Construction supervision

Construction

Provision and maintenance of office equipment

Provision of stationery

Security of offices and other utility premises

Recruitment of staff

Organizational restructuring studies

Legal services

Training of staff

Building repairs and renovation

Vehicle repairs

Outer functions:
- O & M and reading of meters
- O & M communications systems
- O & M pumping stations
- O & M of pipe distribution networks
- O &M of raw water intake
- O & M of water treatment
- O & M of transmission mains
- O & M of bulk water pumping stations
- Provision of tanker supplies
- O & M of sewage treatment
- Water testing
- Sewer cleaning and minor repairs
- O & M of foul pumping stations

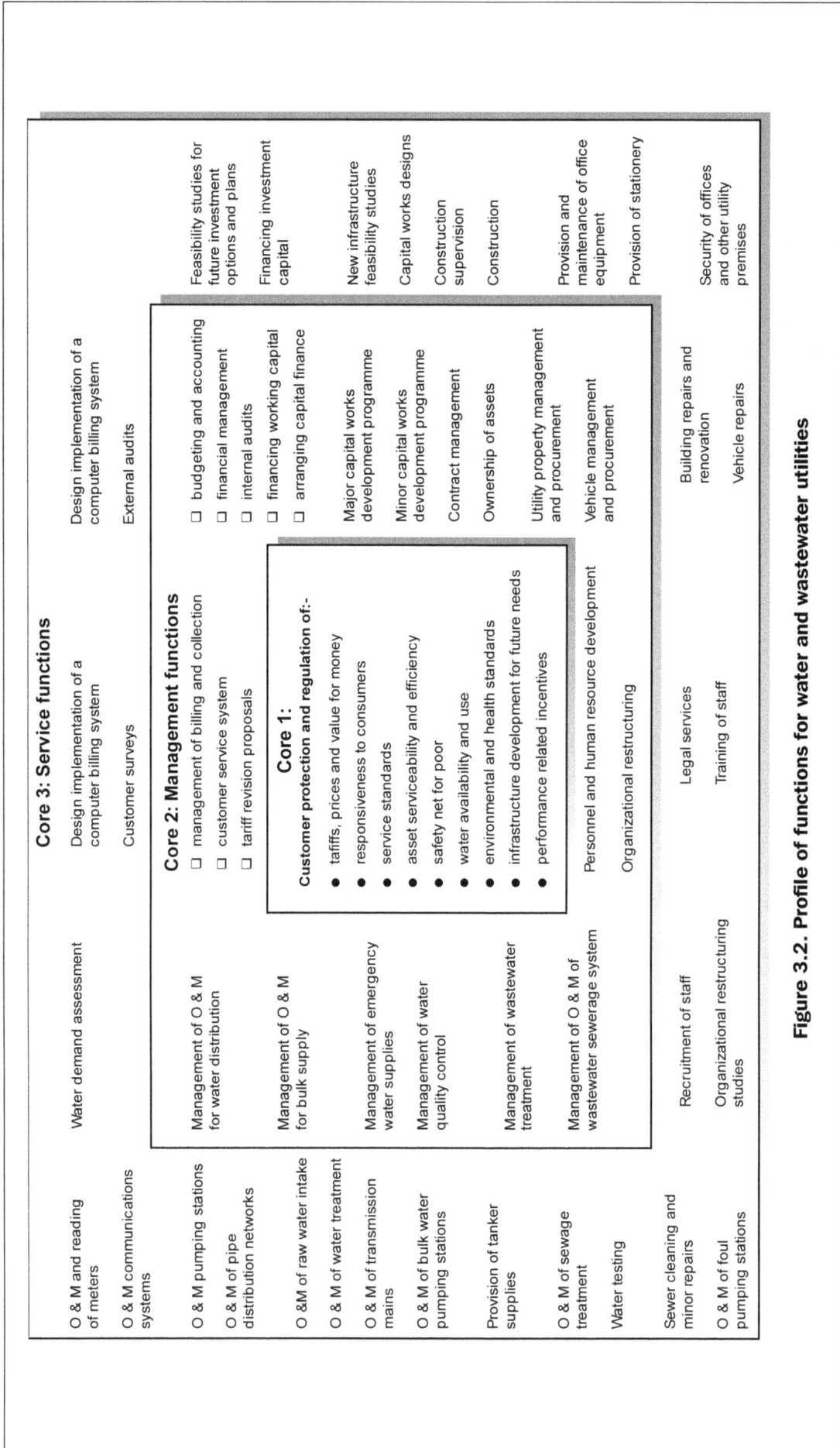

Figure 3.2. Profile of functions for water and wastewater utilities

Retain Improve Outsource Transfer
'California decision tree' Witheford D K, Outsourcing of State Highway Facilities and Services, 1997

PERM Privatise Eliminate Retain Modify

Making Goverment Work: Lessons from America's Governors and Mayors Andrisani & Hakim, 2000

Challenge Compare Consult Compete DETR, 1999

Define the **mission** of the organisation (and hence the essential **responsibilities**)

List the major **activities** of the organisation

Is the activity **necessary** to undertake the organisation's mission and responsibilities?

The contracting out Decision Tree 'Ideal'

No

Yes

Develop measures for cost, quality and delivery (time) of activity (Activity Based Costing) and bench-mark

Is the activity **necessary** to the mission of another organisation within the sector

Is it possible to increase effectiveness and quality or reduce costs by improving work practices?

No

Yes

No

Yes

Periodically review activities against renewed benchmarks to check for improvement opportunities

Transfer activity to appropriate organisation

Cease activity

Yes

Does the organisation have the ability to improve performance of this activity

No

Yes

Improve the performance of the activity

Is direct control essential?

No

No

Is there (or is there potential for) a **competitive market** for contracting out?

Yes

No

Does the organisation have a **comparative advantage**?

Yes

No

Yes

Can the quality be maintained whilst contracting out **part** of the activity

Yes

Investigate how to develop capacity of private sector

Yes

No

Yes

Retain activity

Contract out part of the activity

Contract out the activity

Periodically review activity for contracting out opportunities

Regularly review contracted out activity to determine if cost and quality goals are being achieved and whether contracting-out can be extended

Regularly review contracted out activity to determine if cost and quality goals are being achieved

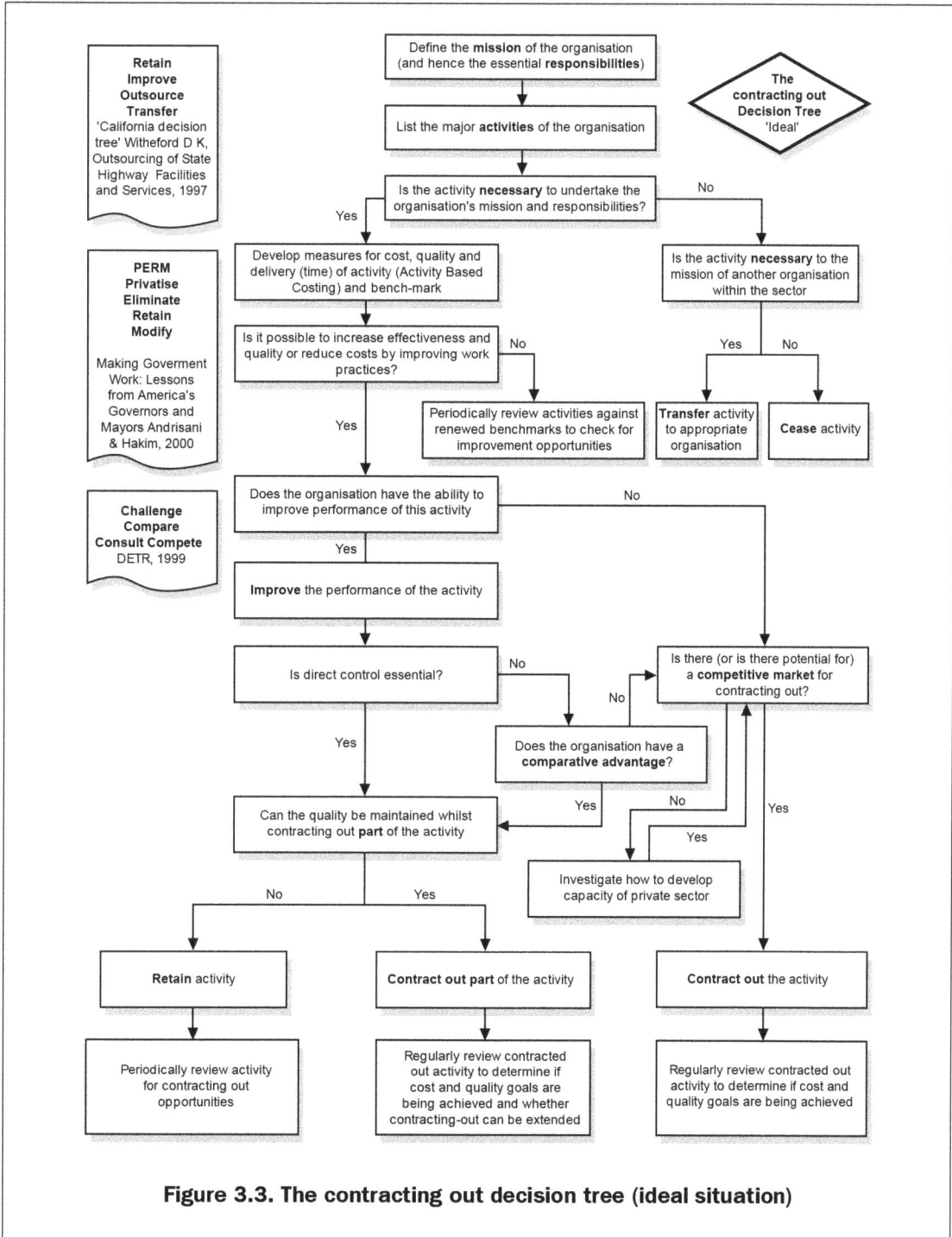

Figure 3.3. The contracting out decision tree (ideal situation)

Define the **mission** of the organisation
(and hence the essential **responsibilities**)

The contracting out Decision Tree 'Realistic'

List the major **activities** of the organisation

Is the activity **necessary** to undertake the organisation's mission and responsibilities?

Yes

No

Develop measures for cost, quality and delivery (time) of activity (Activity Based Costing) and bench-mark

Is the activity **necessary** to the mission of another organisation within the sector

Yes

No

Is it possible to increase effectiveness and quality or reduce costs by improving work practices?

No

Periodically review activities against renewed benchmarks to check for improvement opportunities

Transfer activity to appropriate organisation

Cease activity

Yes

Does the organisation have the ability to improve performance of this activity

No

Yes

Improve the performance of the activity

Is direct control essential?

No

Does the organisation have a **comparative advantage**?

No

Yes

Yes

Is it feasible for government to improve incentives for public providers?

No

Yes

Is it feasible to implement a public sector change programme to improve service?

No

Yes

Will the necessary monitoring process for a public sector change programme, deliver higher benefits than it will cost

No

Is there (or is there potential for) a competitive market for contracting out?

Yes

Retain activity

Contract out the activity

Periodically review activity for contracting out opportunities

Regularly review contracted out activity to determine if cost and quality goals are being achieved

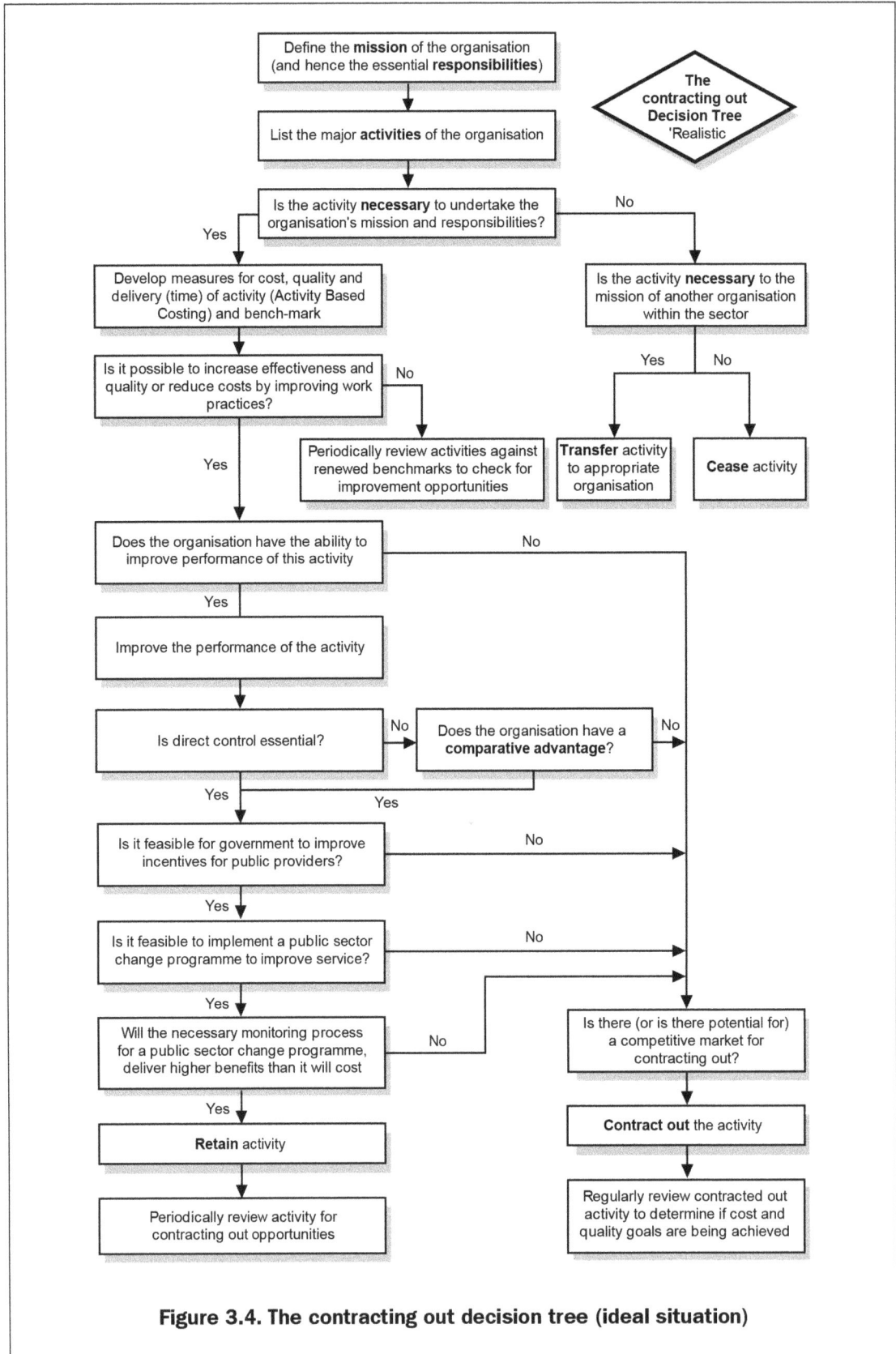

Figure 3.4. The contracting out decision tree (ideal situation)

9.   To reduce the number of public employees and the obligations that go with them, such as pension payments.

10. To inject private investment capital (and improve efficiency in the use of that capital) in order to reduce the predicted public funding shortfall in the sector.

11. To expand service coverage to more customers including the poor.

The extent to which specific benefits can be achieved will, of course, depend on which activities are contracted out and the local enabling environment (which includes social, political, economic and legal conditions). The water utility needs to address critical service provision and cost recovery problems, either within or outside the contract, if poor performance is to be avoided.

The type of contract also has an important bearing on potential benefits. For example, all forms of contract can deliver technical expertise, whereas management, lease and concession contracts can provide improved overall management expertise. The more complex contracts (such as concessions) can potentially provide greater incentives and benefits (particularly objectives 10 and 11 listed above), as more risks are transferred to the operator. The enabling environment needs to be right (such as the utility having the ability to charge adequate tariff levels), for such complex contracts to be successful.

Although management and lease contracts do not usually have capital loan components, such PPP arrangements can attract loans outside the contract. For example, loans from financial institutions, such as the World Bank, to the asset holding company are more likely to be availed where there are well-designed management or lease contracts being developed or in place.

Service and management contracts are attractive because in many cases they are the only achievable PPP options. In addition, they can play an important part in incremental contract development, as discussed in the next section.

Guidance on contract packaging and whether to go for smaller or larger contracts is covered in section 4.2. More specific information on the selection and requirements for each type of contract are also contained in the *Toolkits for Private Participation in Water and Sanitation*, World Bank, 1997.

3.2.2   Advantages and disadvantages of contracting out

According to Lorentzen (1998), the specific advantages and disadvantages of contracting out O&M services are as set out below.

Potential advantages of contracting out

*   Can be cost-effective if there is true competition, prudent procurement procedures and qualified supervision.

*   Puts pressure on the direct labour organization to improve its efficiency.

*   Gives the local authority more flexibility to cope with seasonal variations and other changes in the scale of O&M programme and to respond based on needs rather than based on manpower and equipment at hand.

*   May reduce the authority's management burden, personnel administration and training.

- Can limit the authority's needs for new capital investment in maintenance and equipment.

- Can develop useful benchmarks in terms of cost and performance of O&M and other tasks.

- May provide special skills and innovative methods of work and management.

- Can help develop the local contracting industry, particularly small-scale entrepreneurs

Potential disadvantages of contracting out

- Is not cost-effective if local contracting industry is not truly competitive.

- Demands qualified preparation of tender documents and close and qualified supervision.

- May stimulate fraud and corruption in the procurement process and during supervision.

- May displease civil servants and consequently meet resistance from unions.

- May result in delays if procurement procedures are cumbersome, which is often the case in local authorities in developing countries.

- Increases vulnerability to non-completion of works due to contractors' financial problems, strikes among contractors' personnel etc.

- May lower quality of service to the public because contractors may tend to be less sensitive to the authority's objectives and public demands than civil servants.

- Acceptance of low bids may lead to inferior quality of work.

- Does not provide hands-on experience in the direct labour force so that in-house capabilities may deteriorate.

Many of the potential disadvantages listed above can be minimized through an effective contract development and implementation process that is undertaken with consensus building amongst key stakeholders, in an appropriate enabling environment.

3.2.3 Incremental contract development

If a utility or municipality has not previously contracted out services such as O&M, billing and customer services, one approach (particularly for smaller urban areas) is to experiment with smaller contracts such as service contracts initially, then consider moving onto management and other larger contracts. This will enable the utility to develop its contract management expertise and to test and develop the capabilities of the private sector.

Box 3.4 shows the three-stage sequence of gradual development of service/management contracts initially proposed for the four consortiums serving four areas of Mexico City. This seems a sensible process as information about the system is gathered before moving over to private sector management of the network in stage 3, and the operator's activities can then be properly monitored (Sansom et al, 2003). Unfortunately, the process of moving to stage 3 has been slow in Mexico City, which is in part due to the institutional complexity on the client side, but it still offers a possible model sequence for use elsewhere.

Box 3.4. Incremental contract development in Mexico City [1]

The following three stages on the Mexico City service/management contract represent a systematic sequence—first of gathering information about the network and the customers during stage 1, then the development of customer-orientated tasks in stage 2 and finally moving onto management of O&M during stage 3.

Stage 1 activities — Survey and meter installation tasks (paid by unit price)

- Mapping of the secondary water and drainage networks
- Customer census
- Installation of meters to all customers

Stage 2 activities — Customer-oriented tasks (paid by unit price)

- Meter reading and maintenance
- Billing and collection
- Customer care in dedicated offices
- Bill collection
- Telephone care service
- New connections (water and drainage)

Stage 3 activities — Network management tasks (combined with Stage 2 activities and paid by unit price plus an incentive formula)

- Operation and maintenance of the secondary water and drainage networks
- Detection and repair of visible and non-visible leaks in the potable water networks
- Rehabilitation of water and drainage networks

---

1. Source: Morales-Reyes, Sansom and Franceys, case study in Sansom et al, 2003 (Volume 2)

As they learn from the experience of contracting out services and confidence grows amongst key stakeholders, then more complex contracts, such as lease and concessions, can be considered. Incremental contract development has been successfully implemented in places such as Aguascalientes in Mexico (management to concession contract) and Malindi in Kenya (service to management contract), as detailed in Volume 2 on contracting out case studies (Sansom et al, 2003). A similar approach has also been pursued in cities such as Kampala, Uganda, and Johannesburg, South Africa. In these cases, detailed information about the system and consumers is collected during the management contract phase, which then aids the development of the contract for a concession or lease contract.

The authors acknowledge the argument that small-scale contracting out, even incremental contracting out, can fail to address the underlying issues where utility service failure results from political interference and poor governance. However, noting that private operators presently serve only about 5 per cent of urban areas, we believe that the advantages of 'foreignization,' as seen in the majority of complex PPPs, are unlikely to be extended much beyond the metropolitan areas and their satellites. It is necessary to develop the capacity of national private enterprise so that it will, in time, be able to tender for complex PPPs in secondary towns. Incremental service and management contracts play an important role in this development.

3.2.4 Voluntary competitive tendering

In cases where unions and other stakeholders are resisting contracting out of services, a potential route to be explored is the use of voluntary competitive tendering, where private companies *and* internal public sector workers can bid for contracts let by the public authority. This approach has been followed in the UK, following extensive use of compulsory competitive tendering for local authority services during the 1980s and 1990s.

The major expansion of contracting and competitive tendering in the UK followed the Local Government Act (1988), which required local authorities to subject a range of manual services to competitive tender. If the local authority (through its own direct labour force) won the right to provide the services then it had to do so on a quasi-contractual basis, operating an internal trading account, which could not be cross-subsidized and had to meet stated targets that were set by central government. The services that were initially covered by the act were refuse collection, street cleaning, building cleaning, catering, vehicle maintenance, grounds maintenance and leisure management.' By 1993, 32 per cent of the contracts were being won by the private sector, but this only represented 17 per cent by value as the contractors tended to pick up the smaller contracts and those in local authorities where the authorities were seen to be more in favour of this approach (Walsh, 1995).

Not everything worked perfectly but compulsory competitive tendering (CCT) became a powerful tool to promote change in the public sector. Volume 2 on case studies and contract analysis (Sansom et al, 2003) provides more information on the lessons from CCT. More information can also be obtained from a *Guide to Voluntary Competitive Tendering and Market Testing by Public Authorities*, published in 1998 by the Chartered Institute of Public Finance and Accountancy (CIPFA) in the UK.

3.3 Guiding principles

If the contracts with private companies to provide water and sanitation services are to be more beneficial for all parties, a key area for improvement is the content and the methods used for managing those contracts. The Latham report, *Constructing the Team,* 1994, sets out 13 key principles for developing an effective and fair, modern contract. The Latham report focuses particularly on the construction industry. Contracting out the provision of services for the water sector presents additional challenges.

Building on the Latham concepts, 22 guiding principles have been developed that address key issues related to the development of effective contracts for service provision in the water sector in developing countries. The guiding principles have been categorized under three key contract aspects (A, B, C) and are set out below.

3.3.1 Category A: Guiding principles for contract preparation/process

a) Contracts should be suitably packaged in order to make business sense and attract capable operators.

b) The service to be contracted out should be clearly defined and specified in the contract documents, preferably with a definition of the precise outputs expected from the contracted services.

c) The procedure for tendering and contract award should be transparent and clearly stated prior to the invitation of bids.

d) The bidding process should include an assessment of the tenderer's capability to achieve the project objectives and this should be described in the tender documents.

e) Risks should be identified and allocated to the party best able to manage, estimate and carry the risk.

f) The conditions of contract should be comprehensive and include references to relevant legislation.

g) Contracts should be in an easily comprehensible language with guidance notes where necessary.

h) Key service provision and cost recovery problems should be identified and addressed, either within or outside the contract.

i) Political acceptance and goodwill for the contract should be secured from the key stakeholders.

3.3.2 Category B: Guiding principles for payment aspects

a) Appropriate incentives to encourage successful performance (against carefully chosen indicators and targets that relate to the contract's objectives) should be included in the contract. Redundant incentives (success incentives that are not achievable) should be avoided.

b) Appropriate penalties to discourage poor performance (against carefully chosen indicators and targets that relate to the contract's objectives) should be included in the contract.

c) Flexible means of payment should be included in the contract, such as a management fee, competitive schedule of rates, mobilization payments plus incentives and penalty clauses.

d) The payment process should be specified in the contract, including interim payments, the period within which payments should be made and adjustments for inflation (where necessary). There should be provision for delays in payments and methods of compensation (such as interest) for the delays, including interruption of work or termination of the contract.

e) Open-book accounting for contracted services is desirable as a means of improving transparency, and is an aid to resolving disputes.

f) Appropriate guarantees for the client should be agreed and clearly specified in the contract.

g) Appropriate guarantees for the contractor/operator should be agreed and clearly specified in the contract.

3.3.3 Category C: Guiding principles for partnership aspects

a) The method of financing the contract should be clearly specified.

b) The contract documents should clearly define the roles and duties of all involved. The organization system for implementation of the contract should be specified. There should be separation of roles of Contract Administrator (representing the client), Project Manager (representing the operator) and an independent adjudicator.

c) The contract documents should reflect a specific duty requiring both parties to deal fairly with each other with shared financial motivation and a general presumption to achieve "win-win" solutions to problems that may arise during the course of the contract.

d) The contractor should have autonomy over his own personnel, although minimum requirements for key staff may be stated (such as minimum qualifications and experience).

e) A speedy method of dispute resolution should be clearly set out in the contract documents and an impartial adjudicator acceptable to both parties specified.

f) Provisions for the client's monitoring and evaluation should be included in the contract.

These guiding principles are discussed further in sections 4 to 6 of this document, with example clauses and processes from contracts around the world.

3.4   Typical contract structures

The typical structure for a good service/management contract is listed in Box 3.5 and Box 3.6. Note that it is important to precisely define the scope of works, obligations of each party, penalty and incentive clauses and the payment terms. Utilities developing their own contracts will need to change the clause headings to suite the type and scope of their particular contracts.

The 22 guiding principles, and the more detailed discussion in sections 4, 5 and 6, will also assist in drafting a good contract.

3.5   Services to poor communities

3.5.1   Protecting the interests of the poor

Service and management contracts are very flexible, so in theory it should be relatively easy for the employer or client to ensure that the poor are not disadvantaged through the contract. Four broad ways have been identified through which the interests of the poor can be protected (Brocklehurst and Evans, WSP-SA, 2001). These are briefly discussed with examples below.

1. Pay attention to process

Consultations with the poor can be carried out to find out their preferences for service options and other aspects of the services. NGOs (non-government organizations) and CBOs (community-based organizations) who work with these groups can be useful partners in data collection, or in some cases they can represent the views of community groups. However, unless adequate consultations do take place, the utility/municipality cannot be sure that it is making adequate provision for poorer communities.

Box 3.5. A typical contract structure (Part A)

The following typical structure is based on selected contracts for O&M, billing and collection (continued in Box 3.6)

BACKGROUND
General background
Key objectives
Declarations of main parties

DEFINITIONS AND INTERPRETATIONS
Definitions
Applicable legislation
Authorized representatives
Financial responsibilities and procedures

SCOPE OF WORK
Services under the contract
Standards of performance
Contract duration
Commencement of works
Variations or amendments

OBLIGATIONS, DUTIES OF THE OPERATOR
General scope of work
To deal fairly with all parties
To safeguard, use, manage and control defined assets
To provide O&M services
To manage non-routine and emergency repairs
To charge and collect for services provided
To submit and agree upon work programmes
To submit and agree upon business plans
To maintain and submit accounts
To allow inspection
To maintain and submit records
To provide insurance

---

2. Get the policy environment right

Developing tariff policies and connection charges that do not disadvantage the poor are clear examples of pro-poor policies. If water connection charges are high, then this will act as a disincentive for poorer households to connect. Such charges can be reduced to encourage more connections amongst the poor through measures such as recouping connection costs through water charges. Alternatively, an operator can allow communities or households to contribute their labour in making the pipe connection, in order to reduce the connection costs. This has been successfully done in Buenos Aires.

Many cities do not allow people without official land tenure (for example, in informal settlements) to have water connections, hence land tenure is often a key issue. A potential solution to this problem is for the utility to sell water to community groups who manage their own small pipe network. Payment in such a case may be based on bulk flow meter readings from a meter that is located outside the informal settlement. This is in effect a 'co-operative' type of contract. Such an arrangement has worked successfully in places such as Haiti and Kibera in Nairobi.

Box 3.6. A typical contract structure (Part B)

The following typical structure is based on selected contracts for O&M, billing and collection (continued from Box 3.5)

OBLIGATIONS AND DUTIES OF THE EMPLOYER
General scope
To deal fairly with all parties
Specified retained powers
To set tariffs, fees and charges
To pay a management fee (and other defined fees)
To obtain consents
To audit accounts
Not to interfere with operations (apart from what is stated in contract provisions)

PAYMENT TERMS
Performance security
Payment criteria
Penalties
Incentives
Payment procedures and interim payments
Retention payments
Extraordinary adjustment in fees

BREACH, TERMINATION AND EXPIRATION OF CONTRACTS
Service continuity
Handing over period at end of contract
Termination of contract
Remaining obligations

MISCELLANEOUS
Arbitration
Force Majeure
Indemnity and liabilities
Intellectual property rights

ANNEXES
Payment schedules
Task schedules
Technical details, specifications, etc.

3. Establish robust regulatory structures that are pro-poor

Regulation can be pro-poor through such measures as not allowing private operators exclusive rights to provide water services to particular areas. Small-scale independent providers can therefore continue to provide services to poorly served areas. Operators can also be encouraged to offer different service options in poor areas, such as water kiosks, group connections and yard connections. Encouraging citywide consultation forums can also deal with problems that arise for all consumer groups.

4. Use the contract

General targets for increases in coverage or connections are not usually helpful, as reasons can always be found by the operator not to include hard to reach areas. Targets for improved service levels based on geographical areas where many poor people live in well-defined areas, can be successful. However, funding for any extensions to the pipe network that is needed in poor areas should be specifically arranged, as such capital expenditure is not usually included within service/management contracts.

Specific guidance on making private sector participation work for the poor is given in the Water and Sanitation Program publication (2002) on *New Designs for Water and Sanitation Transactions*. This document examines elements of water sector reform, legal frameworks and making the different forms of PPP contracts work for the poor.

3.5.2 Community/co-operative management contracts

When a utility or water department is considering contracting out water and/or sanitation services, it will usually seek to use capable private contractors. In some cases, however, there are distinct advantages in contracting out to, or working with, community groups/co-operatives for the provision of services, particularly where there are land tenure problems in, for example, informal settlements. This is a means by which a utility can contribute to government poverty reduction strategies.

Volume 2, the contracting out case studies and contract analysis document, (Sansom et al, 2003) provides four brief case studies of successful community management of aspects of water service provision. These are:

- **Haiti:** management of water distribution and the collection of water charges by user associations in Port-Au Prince shanty towns;

- **Kenya:** management of some water distribution pipes and water kiosks by a local CBO in Kibera informal settlement in Nairobi;

- **India:** a sustainable, community-managed, four-village piped water scheme in Kolhapur, Maharashtra; and

- **India:** collection of water charges from customers by community-based groups for the City and Industrial Development Corporation (CIDCO) in New Bombay.

Some of the key factors for a utility to consider when contemplating contracting out services to community groups or collaborating with them are listed below.

- Are there community or user groups who are able and willing to take on the management of distinct service provision tasks?

- Do the groups have the necessary skills to undertake the identified tasks, or are there clear opportunities for them to develop their capacities to the required level?

- Consideration should be given as to where the community groups have a 'comparative advantage' over other management arrangements. For example, if a community group wants to manage O&M and/or cost recovery for water services in their own informal settlement, they have the advantage of understanding what is and what is not acceptable in that community. In addition, they are likely to be competitive in terms of labour costs in their own area, because where they want to improve services for themselves and their neighbours, they do not have to incur travel costs.

- When negotiating with community groups, it may be easier and more effective to use an intermediary or facilitator, perhaps from an NGO, who has suitable communication skills and experience of working with such communities.

- To minimize the cost of monitoring and evaluation of the work of community groups, it is best to keep matters simple wherever possible. This can be achieved by having easily measurable indicators for success and simple payment terms. For example, indicators of success may be the number of working water kiosks and connections, as well as the prices they charge as compared to vendor prices. The payment terms for, say, a community group managing the water distribution system in their area, could be based on readings of the bulk flow meter on the water main that supplies their pipe network.

Chapter 4

Contract preparations and processes

Water utilities or municipalities wishing to contract out services should design contracts around the identified needs of the customer and effective service provision, and not simply a codification of the service that has been historically provided. The specification should, as far as possible, be defined in terms of outputs, including targets for improved service provision. Guidance on contract preparations and developing appropriate processes are provided in the following sections.

The flowchart in Figure 4.1 sets out the key stages in the contracting out process. Note that consensus building with key stakeholders needs to be considered for each stage. It is recommend that a contract(s) committee be established to streamline decision making and to monitor progress of contract development. It is also beneficial to engage capable consultants to advise on the contract development process.

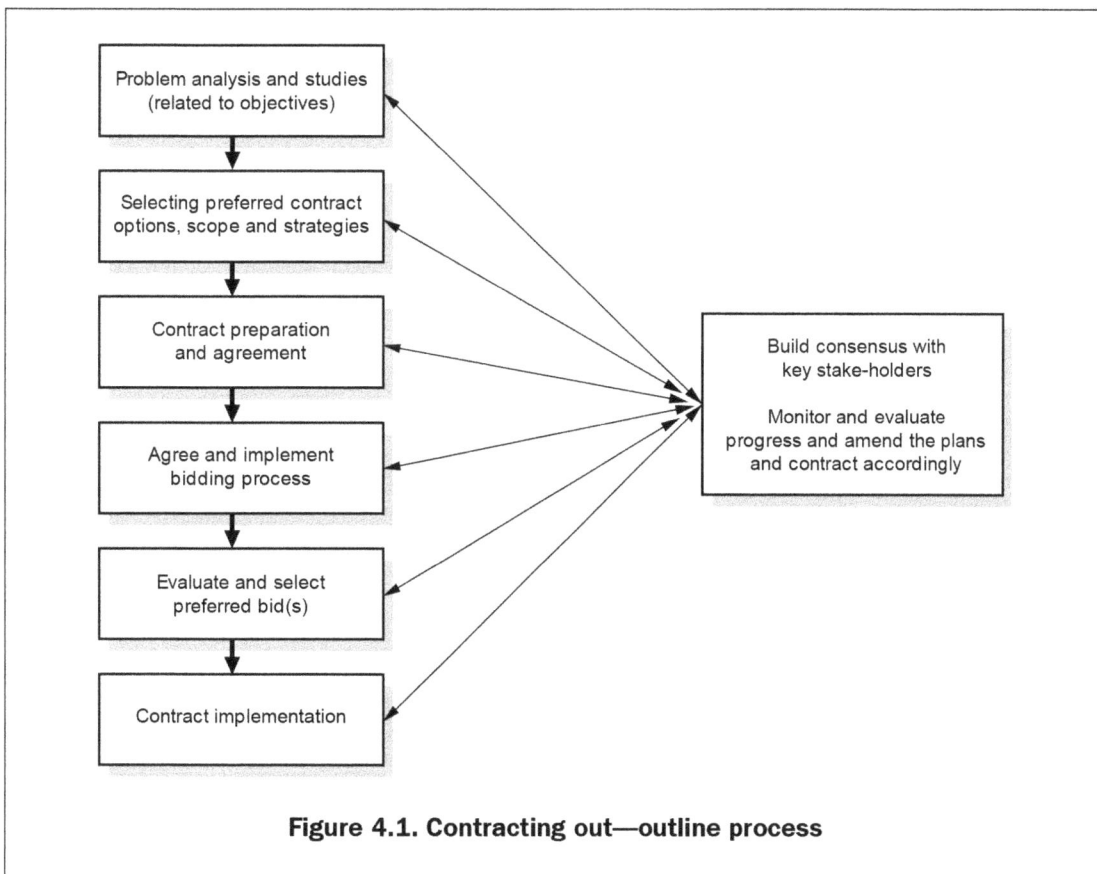

Figure 4.1. Contracting out—outline process

4.1   Addressing key problems

Guiding principle: Key service provision and cost recovery problems should be identified and addressed either within or outside the contract.

If contracting out is to have significant impacts on service provision or cost recovery, then critical problems need to be addressed, either within or outside the contract. A common problem in the sector is the review of water tariffs and the approval of increases. For contracts involving cost recovery, an inability by the client water utility to review and increase tariffs, may lead to problems for the contractor to generate adequate funds for sustaining water services. This could result in the termination of the contract. This problem was the main cause of the termination of a service contract in Malindi, Kenya. Similar problems were experienced in Trinidad and Tobago—refer to Box 4.1 for a brief discussion of these cases, as well as the constraints encountered on the Kampala contract.

Box 4.1. Contract examples where key problems were not fully addressed

Malindi service contract [1]
For the Malindi O&M and billing service contract in Kenya in the mid-1990s, one of the objectives of the contract was to generate adequate funds to meet operations and maintenance costs, as well as to eventually meet the operator's fees. However, the client water utility was unable to increase tariffs, and this led to a situation where the revenue collected could not finance the contract without external support. When external support for the contract ceased, the water utility could not meet the operator's fees and the contract lapsed. The client water utility reverted to direct provision of services. There was a decline in the level of water services (including revenue collection) soon after the private operator left. The contract could not be sustained because one of the critical service provision problems had not been addressed.

Trinidad and Tobago contract [2]
The private operator (Trinidad and Tobago Water Services) achieved improvements in a number of key areas during the management contract (1996–99). However, the government was not entirely satisfied and did not proceed to the next phase of the contract. Improvements in service provision were hampered because tariffs had not been increased sufficiently and the proposed World Bank loan was not forthcoming. Hence, the renewal of the contract was adversely affected by the lack of a 'willingness to charge' higher water rates. This case emphasizes the need to deal with all the key constraints in the management of a utility.

Kampala KRIP contract [3]
In the Kampala case study, the main objective of the Kampala Revenue Improvement Project (a management contract) was to improve revenue collection in Kampala. While the client water utility had improved the production capacity at the treatment plant, the city's water distribution network had not been upgraded to the degree necessary for it to be able to increase the number of customers. The contractor could only realise modest improvements in revenue because the critical service provision problem had not been addressed.

---

1. Njiru and Sansom, case study in Sansom et al, 2003)
2. *Sansom et al, Volume 2, 2003)*
3. *Mugisha and Franceys, case study in Sansom et al, 2003)*

Key lesson that emerge from the contracting out case studies and contract analyses are listed below.

- There is a greater chance of successful contract outcomes where there is an effective commercial orientation in the water utility as well as in the contractor/operator. This is evident from countries such as Chile as well as many others.

- Thorough studies are required to obtain information about the condition of the infrastructure and the service levels provided. Only then can contract performance can be accurately measured.

- Cost recovery and water tariff issues need to be addressed early in the contract development stage, so that there will be adequate funding to support the performance levels that are envisaged.

4.2   Contract packaging and development

Guiding Principle: Contracts should be suitably packaged in order to make business sense and attract capable operators.

Contractors or operators exist to meet various business aims, just as government departments exist to meet their objectives. It is important to package work in such a way that it makes sense to the business community, while also meeting the objectives of the utility. Contracts that are not packaged appropriately may fail to attract suitable and capable contractors. Appropriate packaging of contracts calls for judgements about:

1. How far the work should be subdivided into different smaller contracts, for example for different areas or different specializations; and

2. Whether to package the work into combined larger contracts including a number of different activities.

Choosing option 1—subdividing work into smaller contracts—may be done for a number of reasons, including:

- to begin to experiment with contracting out, allowing the utility and the private sector to learn through the experience of managing contracts with only limited risks;

- to allow local operators/contractors to bid and gain more expertise; and

- to increase competition if there are concerns about the number of potential bidders for larger contracts.

The selection of option 2—to package the work into combined larger contracts—is likely to be done for two main reasons.

- To increase commercial incentives, particularly where there are potential 'synergies' between related activities. For example, to combine O&M, billing and customer services in one management or lease contract can enable the provision of strong incentives for improving all three activities. This can be achieved giving the operator small percentage incentive payments related to improved cost recovery. The operator will therefore be motivated to improve all of its activities, including O&M and customer services, to keep customers satisfied and hence increase their willingness to sustain payments.

- To realize more substantial benefits from contracting out by maximizing the amount of utility activities that are contracted out within one contract provides more commercial incentives for the operator to improve services and reduce costs across the whole range of activities. This is particularly true where 'economies of scale' can be used on larger contracts. If the enabling environment is supportive, then more complex contracts, such as concessions and lease contracts, should be considered, particularly if potential benefits are to be maximized.

Contract packaging can have a major influence on the level of interest from contractors and on the extent of competition that will result. In general, greater competition leads to lower prices. Therefore, only when utilities have evidence that economies of scale or greater competition will result from contract amalgamation should such contracts be pursued (Audit Commission, 1993). Judgements about contract packaging are best made on a case-by-case basis, bearing in mind the reasons for choosing option 1 or 2 as discussed above. This is a matter on which expert consultants and operators can provide useful advice.

During the process of contract development, some of the key issues that need to be resolved include:

- Who owns the assets and who can let the contract?

- What are the objectives and scope of the contract?

- What are the procedures for making key decisions about the contract?

- What is the area to be served?

- Will the service area be split up into a number of contracts to encourage competition between operators?

- What will be the duration of the contract?

- How should responsibilities be allocated between private and public stakeholders?

- Who will be responsible for capital expenditure? (Note: this is not usually included in service/management contracts, although specific provisions can be drafted for this purpose).

- Who will distinguish between routine maintenance and capital expenditure and how will both types of work be measured and paid for?

- What will be the operator's environmental liabilities?

- How will unpredicted costs be dealt with under the contract?

- What technical information will be given to bidders, including an inventory of assets? (Note: the more quality information that is available, the better).

- What factors would allow the employer/client to extend the contract? (Note: extensions to short-term contracts are not normally necessary, except where there have been significant delays outside the control of the operator).

Such issues should, hopefully, be resolved early in the contract development process to avoid potential delays and redrafting later.

4.3 Specifications and outputs

Guiding Principle: The services to be contracted out should be clearly defined and specified in the contract documents, preferably with a definition of the precise outputs expected from the contracted services.

The objectives and standards of the service to be provided should be clearly stated in the contract. The logic is that unless and until it is clear why we do things, it is impossible to specify how that service can be most cost-effectively provided (UK Government multi-department review, 1986).

The nature of the specification has a major impact on the administrative costs of a contract (Audit Commission, 1993). The three main elements to be considered are:

* inputs, which specify the resources (human, physical and financial) that are to be used;

* processes, which define the tasks and methods that will be undertaken; and

* outputs, which describe the services and results that the customers or client will receive.

The emphasis on each of these elements in the specification will depend on which services are to be contracted out. However, it is recommended that, as far as possible, outputs should be specified rather than inputs and processes. Specifications should start with a definition of the outputs expected from the contracted service. An output-focused specification can be more flexible, require less administrative effort and should provide greater value for money for the contracting utility than one focused on inputs or processes. It also gives contractors more room for innovation that may enhance efficiency and effectiveness. The specification is likely to include references to relevant legislation that the operator will need to comply with. Detailed specification of the requirement is essential, but how to deliver that requirement should be left to the contractor, so that he or she has every incentive to introduce new techniques. Over-specifying restricts the contractors' scope to innovate, to take advantage of economies of scale or to employ standard methods and materials.

4.4 Management of risks

Guiding Principle: Risks should be identified and allocated to the party best able to estimate, manage and carry those risks.

A common tendency of public sector water departments is to assume that the social obligation to provide adequate and reliable water and sewerage services is the exclusive role of the public sector. In such situations there is often reluctance to hand over responsibilities and risks to the private sector, even when contractors are used for some aspects of service provision. Box 4.2 highlights an example where the client was reluctant to allow a private operator to manage risks at the Temghar water works in India. The public sector can, of course, ensure that the public is well served by careful contract development, appointing competent operators and by making adequate regulation arrangements.

A clear allocation of risk is required to avoid confusion and disputes. so that there is little or no argument over financial ownership of a particular problem, and it is therefore clear who should take action to prevent such a problem occurring or minimize its impact if it does (Broome J, 1999).

In general terms, private operators are best able to manage construction and operating risks due to their greater flexibility. The public sector, on the other hand, is better at bearing risks such as delays in obtaining permission and political risks, because of its greater influence. A more detailed assessment of risks for different contracts is outlined in the World Bank's *Toolkits for Private Participation in Water and Sanitation*, 1997.

**Box 4.2. Reluctance to transfer risks
— Temghar service contract, India [1]**

The scope of this service contract, which was let each year from 1993 to 2000, included O&M of a raw water pumping station, a 210 Mld capacity treatment plant, a pure water pumping station and a power sub-station at Temghar. The contract sum covered only the minor repairs, but included labour costs for major repairs for a period of one year. In case of major repairs, all materials were to be supplied by the client (MJP).

The work of the contractor was directed by the client's (MJP's) engineer-in-charge on a daily basis and the duties of each of the contractor's staff was specified in the contract. Hence, there was very limited scope for the contractor to introduce his own improvements and cost savings. MJP supervised the contract in a detailed manner with a qualified supervisory staff of 3 engineers and 22 labourers. Such high client staffing levels indicates a lack of willingness to delegate management to the private contractors, or perhaps there was a reluctance to reduce or redeploy staff. Such intensive supervision also raises doubts about the overall cost-effectiveness of the contract.

There were no incentives in the contract to encourage the contractor to improve performance. However, there were a number of penalty clauses that generally related to absenteeism of staff and not carrying out specified duties. The contract was, in effect, a labour-only contract, where the contractor provided the staff to perform specific duties, but where very little risk was passed on to the contractor. It was reported that adequate policy support was not available in 1999 from the state government to make any major amendments to the ongoing contract, although more recently there appears to be a greater willingness to change and pursue other contract options.

---

1. *Gawade and Sansom, case study (1998), in Sansom et al, 2003*

4.5   Comprehensive conditions of contract

Guiding principle: The conditions of contract should be comprehensive to minimize the potential for disputes.

The conditions of contract should be sufficiently comprehensive to enable effective execution and regulation of that contract. Contract conditions provide the framework for service delivery and should not change for the duration of the contract. Contract conditions should clearly answer the eight key questions that are set out in Box 4.3. These questions need to be addressed in a comprehensive manner that minimizes the potential for disputes during the execution of the contract.

Box 4.3. Essential questions to be answered by the contract conditions [1]

- Who are the parties to the contract?
- What are the powers and responsibilities of these parties?
- When and how does the contract come into effect?
- How are changes to be made to the specification?
- What are the arrangements for making payments, including interim payments?
- What happens when things go wrong?
- What provisions are there for events outside the control of the contract parties?
- What happens at the end of the contract?

---

1. Source: Audit commission, 1993

The contract conditions should define the procedures for corrective action if contractors under-perform, with such action appropriate to the level of failure. Service delivery problems should be resolved at the lowest possible level, but there should be procedures available to resolve problems at a higher level or at arbitration.

Increasingly, contracts such as the Institution of Civil Engineers Professional Services Contract, NEC document, in the UK, are designed to encourage a partnership approach between the parties to the contract, so that win-win outcomes emerge. This way of managing contract relationships has also been used elsewhere, for example, in countries such as Mexico. Contract conditions that enable such an approach are more likely to lead to mutually beneficial contracting out of services.

4.6   Use of clear and comprehensible language

Guiding principle: Contracts should be drafted in an easily comprehensible language with guidance notes where necessary.

When preparing new bid documents, engineering departments tend to adapt old contracts that may have old-fashioned 'legal language.' Often such language is not entirely clear to the people responsible for executing the contracts. A contract is an important management tool that should be clear and organized for effective communication.

The terms used in the contract should be clearly explained to avoid ambiguity, with guidance notes where necessary. Contracts drawn up in an easily comprehensible language will potentially avoid disputes resulting from different interpretations of those contracts. It is, therefore, preferable to develop new contract documents, where appropriate, with clear and unambiguous language, so that misunderstandings are minimized.

It is also important that contracts are laid out logically and that the cross-references in the document make sense. A worthwhile exercise is to ask an independent person to review all the contract documents to ensure that it is clear and concise with no ambiguities, before the tender invitations are sent out.

4.7   Clear procedures for tendering and contract award

Guiding principle: The procedures for tendering and contract award should be transparent and clearly stated prior to the invitation of bids.

Contracts for the management of water services have been awarded in some countries on the basis of negotiations with a single operator. There are considerable doubts about whether such arrangements deliver value for money. An effective, competitive tendering process is a vital part of contracting out, both in terms of choosing the most suitable bidder and minimizing costs., It is therefore, generally recommended that competitive tendering be adopted as much as possible.

Where procedures for tendering and contract award are clear, transparent and comprehensive, the more able and experienced contractors and joint ventures are more likely to submit competitive bids. The contract letting (tendering) procedures should be as transparent as possible. The utility should define and adhere to a timetable, provide relevant information to all potential tenderers, carry out tender evaluation fairly and utilize the mobilization period to resolve anticipated difficulties (Audit Commission, 1993). Where the client provides good information about the infrastructure and services to be managed as part of the contract, the likelihood of competitive bids being submitted is also increased. The client should also include in the bid documents details of facilities that will be made available to the contractor.

Box 4.4. Johannesburg management contract tendering timetable [1]

1. Consultants appointed by council committee to draft tender documents (October 1999).

2. Invitations for pre-qualification (expression of interest) sent out (December 1999).

3. A total of seven joint ventures of leading companies were pre-qualified to bid (February 2000).

4. The request for proposals was issued to the selected tenderers (June 2000).

5. Five tenders were received, including technical and financial proposals (September 200).

6. The technical evaluation report was prepared. Only those bidders who scored a technical rating of more than 75 per cent were considered as part of the financial assessment (October 2000).

7. The advisory board and council committee discussed both the technical report and financial proposals and the preferred bidder was selected (November 2000).

8. The contract became operational in April 2001.

---

1. Source: A. Still, GJMC, 2001

The tendering procedure and timetable of the Greater Johannesburg water management contract is set out in Box 4.4. This is an appropriate process for medium to large contracts relating to the provision of services.

Key decisions to be taken in the bidding process include:

a) the information to be provided to bidders and the form it will take;

b) the extent to which there will be discussions with bidders before the formal bidding begins, and the form these discussions will take;

c) the instructions to bidders on what their proposals should contain;

d) the rules and scoring mechanisms that will be used to evaluate bids;

e) how complaints and appeals will be handled; and

f) the timetable for the bidding.

Source: World Bank, Toolkits for private participation in water and sanitation (1997)

Competitive tendering and contracting out require commercial skills, including procurement and contract management, which are often in short supply in public organizations. It is for this reason that public water utilities should seriously consider the use of independent and experienced consultants for contract development. The objective of an efficient tendering procedure is to buy a long-term business relationship that will depend on trust as much as on legality. This requires both commercial judgements in choosing the contractor and skill and determination in obtaining value for money from the contract.

Table 4.1 shows the main stages recommended for tendering and contract award in Mexico. Note that on receipt of the bids, the technical proposals are opened and evaluated, while the financial proposals (price offers) remain closed. This allows an objective decision on the technical proposals to be made.

Only those bids whose technical proposals have passed proceed to the opening of the financial proposals.

Even where it is government policy to only accept the lowest bid, it is recommended that an assessment be carried out to determine if the lowest bid is realistically priced. In some cases the lowest bid is far below the average bid, which may imply that the lowest bidder cannot achieve the specified contract objectives without incurring substantial losses. In Mexico, the law specifies the requirement to assess the adequacy of the lowest bid price or the 'solvency' of the bid. An example of provisions for assessing the adequacy of lower bids is set out in Box 4.5, together with the key steps for making the assessment.

Note that some activities listed in Table 4.1 (the Mexican example) can be carried out concurrently to reduce time. For example, the feasibility studies and the market assessment of known and interested contractors, can be carried out at the same time.

In Mexico, the technical evaluation results are generally pass or fail; no weighting is allowed in the published bid evaluation decisions. In other countries, such as Uganda and

Table 4.1. Typical process for contract award in Mexico [1]

Stage in the process	Time (weeks)	Key issues
1. System performance studies and feasibility analysis	12–40	To document an assessment of the area related to the contract, define contract objectives and means of payment.
2. Market assessment for contractors	3–8	Review of known contractors to assess their capacity to cope with the contract objectives.
3. Decision on type of tender	1–2	Whether it is a bid invitation from a select list of contractors, or an open national or an open international invitation. (In Mexico this usually depends on the estimated value of the contract).
4. Development of bidding documents and contract	3–10	It is recommended that the utility use expert advice for the development of the contract, and set up a contract committee for key decisions and to review progress.
5. Publication of bid invitation and selling of documents	1	Publication in newspapers and related Webpages. (Personal invitation if select tenders was decided) [2].
6. Pre-qualification of tenderers	1–2	Bid publication may require a pre-qualification of tenderers. Specified criteria and weighting is recommended.
7. Proposal development by bidders, visits and questions	4–12	In this phase the committee is answering questions from the bidders and organizing visits. Changes to the tender documents can be made at this stage, provided such changes are agreed by all parties, including the bidders.
8. Open technical bids; start of technical evaluation	2–5	The committee begins the technical evaluation. Specified criteria and weighting is recommended. Bidders may be contacted by the committee to clarify their proposals.
9. Technical proposal decision takes place; financial (price) evaluation commences	2–5	The technical bid evaluations are finalized and the financial offers of those who have 'passed' the technical stage are opened and presented to all tenderers. [3].
10. Contract assignment	1	The committee awards the contract on the basis of the lowest bid offer. [4].
11. Contract signature and commencement	3–6	The final contract draft is discussed between parties and guarantees are agreed prior to signing.

1. The range of estimated times in weeks that are shown in the table are for a small service contract (1–2 years) and a medium sized management contract (5–7 years)
2. A payment by the bidder is usually required as a guarantee of the tenderer's seriousness to remain in the process up to the decision phase.
3. In Mexico the technical evaluation results are generally pass or fail; no weighting is allowed in the published bid evaluation decisions. This is probably intended to minimize collusion.
4. Before awarding the contract to the lowest bidder, it is important to check that the bid is not too low and unrealistically priced, with a risk that the contractor will not be able to fulfil the contract obligations. Refer to Box 4.5 for guidance in assessing the lowest bids. (Source: Morales-Reyes, 2004)

South Africa, a combined weighting assessment of both the technical and financial proposals has been used on management contracts for the water sector.

Experience in Mexico (Morales-Reyes, J.I., 2004) has shown that insisting on key issues such as those outlined in box 14, has led to the submission of better proposals over time. It is evident that this process assists with the learning curve of new companies.

Box 4.5. Assessing the lowest bids—an example from Mexico [1]

As part of the contract feasibility analysis, the current costs of providing the services to be contracted out should be calculated (a pre-tender estimate) and used as a benchmark for assessing the bid prices. Some key points on assessing financial proposals are set out below.

A) FINANCIAL PROVISIONS TO INCLUDE IN THE BIDDING DOCUMENTS

1. The format for the financial proposals should include all the payment items in the contract. For example, the format should include fixed management fees, plus variable fees such as payment per M3 of water treated, plus any schedules of rates.

2. Provide basic financial formats for the bidders that include a calculation of the total fees (fixed and variable) for one year's operation. This is to be completed by each bidder and submitted with their tender. This calculation will be useful in comparing the financial bids.

3. Request that the bidders split the major components of their proposed fees such as: direct staff, material and equipment costs, overheads, taxes and profit. (This can be useful for bidding comparison and for dealing with disputes later on).

4. Request that the bidders provide electronic copies of their financial bid breakdowns to facilitate easy bid comparison.

B) ASSSESSING THE ADEQUACY AND CORRECTNESS OF THE LOWEST BIDS:

The assessment of the financial bids includes the following key steps, assuming that the remaining bidders have 'passed' the technical appraisal.

1. Open financial bids in front of the bidders and compare fee totals.

2. Analyse the bid breakdowns, preferably using electronic copies provided by the bidders. Note: incentive and penalty clauses are not considered at this stage.

3. Prepare a tender assessment report that includes aspects such as:

- The total fee figures (for one year's operation) for each bid, from lowest to highest.

- A summary of the breakdown of each bidder's fees, noting any discrepancies.

- A note of any errors in the proposals, and whether or not the relevant bidder is prepared to 'stand by its total bid price' (which should not change) after the correction(s) has been made. (If not, then it should be withdrawn from the process).

- Documentation of the average bid figure plus the percentage difference between each bid.

- If the difference between the lowest bid and the second lowest or average bid is substantial, (say more than 20 per cent) then a judgement needs to be made about whether the lowest bidder can achieve the contract objectives for their quoted price and whether their bid should be accepted or rejected. It is also useful to make a comparison with the pre-tender estimate.

- Prepared and signed minutes of all meetings with bidders, including them in the respective proposals.

4. The contract committee will then need to review the tender assessment report and decide which tender it should accept. Note, it is usual to accept the lowest bid, provided it is believed that the lowest bidder can achieve the contract objectives for their quoted price.

1. Adapted from Finagua SC 'Contracting and Finance for Water and Reuse.'Internal document 2001

The improvement of documents submitted over time throughout several contract processes has also shown that bidding documents and draft contracts are a good media to spread good standards and knowledge, and to develop capacities of the sector and the newer companies.

The reasons for having a rigorous procedure such as the one shown for Mexico include being able to:

- select a successful bidder who is able to meet the contract objectives at a reasonable price;

- ensure transparency and maintain confidence in the legitimacy of the process amongst the stakeholders;

- obtain competitive bids at market prices;

- minimize corruption and collusion between bidders; and

- minimize corruption and collusion between bidders and the committee who is awarding the contract.

4.8   Assessment of the capability of tenderers

Guiding principle: The bidding process should include an assessment of the tenderer's capability to achieve the project objectives and this should be described in the tender documents.

The benefits of competitive tendering can only be realized if the competing firms are capable of carrying out the contracted works. It is therefore important for the water utility to assess and confirm the capability of each firm during the bidding process. This may be achieved initially through a pre-qualification process whereby interested firms are required to demonstrate their capability before being invited to submit formal proposals. Typical criteria that can be used to assess the capability of bidders at the pre-qualification stage include:

- relevant experience of the companies' key personnel;

- efficiency and performance on recent projects or franchises;

- accounting histories and financial trends (such as their net profits over the last 3 years and details of their assets and liabilities);

- financial references or bank guarantees of the main bidding companies.

An example of criteria used at the pre-qualification stage on a meter-reading contract in Chile is shown in Box 4.6.

At the bid evaluation phase, the technical proposals are best assessed against agreed criteria such as:

- the quality of the proposals or business plan for managing the contract;

- relevant experience of the key personnel who the bidding company is proposing work on the project;

- the letters confirming collaboration by the members of the bid consortium; and

- other issues important to the client.

Box 4.6. Chile EMOS meter reading contract—pre-qualification [1]

Pre-qualification of tenderers is based on the following criteria and weightings:

Criteria	Weighting
Experience of staff	0.3
Past contract performance	0.4
Financial capacity	0.3

The bidders are asked to complete questionnaires, which are designed to assess performance against these criteria. The pre-qualification committee then assesses each bidder using a scoring system of 1 = insufficient (which implies elimination of the company), 2 = regular, 3 = better than regular and 4 = good. A certain number of companies are then allowed to proceed to the tender stage.

---

1. Source: Morale-Reyes and Franceys, case study, in Sansom et al, 2003

The technical proposals can either be assessed using a scoring system where each bidder must achieve a score of, say, 70 per cent if their financial proposal envelopes are to be opened. Or the evaluation committee can just decide if the technical proposals have either passed or failed their requirements. Alternatively, the client can merely rely on its assessment of the technical capability of the bidders at the pre-qualification stage. The evaluation procedures should comply with local laws and regulations.

4.9   Political acceptance and the support of stakeholders

Guiding principle: Political acceptance and goodwill for the contract should be secured from the key stakeholders.

The water sector has many stakeholders, such as politicians and unions, who have the potential to influence the success or failure of contracts. It is therefore recommended that such stakeholders be fully consulted during the process of reforms and contract development. When dealing with unions, for example, it is worthwhile developing a communications strategy (perhaps together with potential operators) to allay the unions' fears about aspects such as:

a) the numbers of expected compulsory redundancies;

b) voluntary redundancy packages;

c) conditions of service for staff who are transferred to the private operator; and

d) what will happen to transferred staff at the end of the contract?

As the urban water and sanitation sector in developing countries is an expanding industry, there should only be a limited number of compulsory redundancies. Where this is a particular problem, redeployment options can be explored. Competent private operators will value good staff and will therefore seek to provide attractive remuneration packages, provided there is enough scope in the contract for the operator to generate sufficient revenues.

It is worthwhile familiarizing any key politicians and other key stakeholders with the objectives and arrangements of proposed contracts, as well as addressing their concerns. This could be done through means such as study tours to other contracts, presentations and meetings. Where proposed contracts compliment the policies of leading political parties, there is a much better chance of avoiding political interference. The use of voluntary competitive tendering, mentioned in section 3.2.2, can also be considered as a means of reducing the resistance of key stakeholders to contracting out services.

Where some of the stakeholders are not giving their full support, judgements need to be made about whether or not to proceed. It may be that those groups who doubt the value of the proposed contract can be convinced at a later date. Service and management contracts tend to be less controversial amongst stakeholders than more complex contracts, such as concessions. This is because they are of a shorter duration and less authority is transferred to the private sector.

Chapter 5

Payments, incentives and penalties

5.1   Flexible means of payment

Guiding principle: *Flexible means of payment should be included in the contract, such as a management fee, competitive schedule of rates, mobilization payments plus incentives and penalty clauses, where appropriate.*

The use of different and flexible means of payment to cover a variety of eventualities, reduces the risk of the operator claiming he or she has not been paid for legitimate work. Box 5.1 shows the different components of the management fee for Ugandan small towns management contracts in 2001. Payment on such a basis is a way of ensuring fair payment for actual work done. Such fee components can also act as incentives for the operator to diligently complete individual tasks.

Another useful fee component that can be used if required is a 'training fee' that is paid after verification of satisfactory completion of training. This provides reassurance to the client that new or transferred members of staff have received relevant training.

In the case of minor construction works or major/urgent repairs that are not allowed for in management fees in the contract, the use of a priced schedule of rates provides a flexible alternative means of payment. The operator or contractor should price or agree to a schedule of rates or prices for a list of standard items of work, based on assumed quantities. The client can then ask the operator to undertake such minor or emergency works when the need arises and use the schedule of rates to pay the operator. For larger pieces of work that fall outside the contract, separate tenders can be invited, but of course this takes time and is not always suitable for emergency works.

Mobilization payments are sometimes needed by operators to assist them in managing their cash flow while they provide staff and resources in readiness for taking over a particular service. However, this is less likely to be necessary where there is a base fee, as in the Ugandan fee structure.

A more simplified means of payment is shown in Box 5.2 for a draft comprehensive management contract in Bulgaria. In choosing an appropriate means of paying the operator, in conjunction with the incentive and penalty clauses, a number of factors should be considered. These include:

Box 5.1. Ugandan small towns contracts—breakdown of monthly fees[1]

The monthly fee paid to the operators for the water supply management contracts let in 2001 are calculated on the following basis:

1. **Base fee (shillings per month)**—the fixed component that the client agrees to pay to the operator each month to cover the operator's fixed general costs, administrative costs and overheads, plus a reasonable mark-up.

2. **Water sales fee (shillings per m3)**— the component the client agrees to pay the operator to cover production costs for water sold, plus a reasonable mark-up.

3. **Billing fee (shillings per connection per month)**—the component paid to cover the costs of servicing customers, plus a reasonable mark-up.

4. **Pipe network maintenance fee (shillings per km)**—the component the client pays the operator to cover the cost of routine maintenance of the pipe network, plus a reasonable mark-up.

5. **New connections fee (shillings per connection)**—the amount the client pays the operator to cover the costs of making new connections, plus a reasonable mark-up.

6. **Total monthly fee—the** amount determined by adding up components 1 to 5.
   Note: the fee rate for each component is based on the amounts entered into the preferred bid, with reference to the assumed quantities that were estimated by the client for the first two years of operation. Minor extensions to the pipe network are paid for based on the client's agreement to the operator's business plan and proposals.

---

1. Source: Republic of Uganda's standard management contract for small towns, 2001.

- What are the best means of encouraging the operator to meet the client's objectives?

- Is the proposed means of payment fair to both parties? and

- Is the verification of the proposed means of payment relatively straightforward and likely to minimise disputes?

The payment terms for each potential contract needs to be considered on a case-by-case basis, bearing in mind the above criteria.

Box 5.2. Bulgaria contract—components of operator's fees[1]

This draft comprehensive management contract for water and sewerage, including billing and collection, has the following relatively simple payment mechanism. Note that this means of payment also acts an incentive for good performance and a disincentive for poor performance.

1. Annual management allowance

This allowance will be paid on the number of cubic metres of water sold during the year.

2. Annual bonus on returns

This bonus is determined on the basis of the income and expenses in the operating account (open book accounting).

---

1. *Source: Safege consulting engineers, London Economics, Lyonaise des Eaux, Interim report, 1993*

In Mexico, most contracts for operation and maintenance of sewerage treatment plants have two components (Morales-Reyes, 2003). Each one includes unit costs as specified below.

- The fixed fee. This component is a base monthly fee where the fixed components are summed. The fixed components are those that are not related to the flow of water or sewage, for example, personnel, the cost of installations, overheads, insurance and taxes).

- The variable fee. This component is a unitary fee multiplied by the volume treated. This unitary fee is obtained in the proposal by dividing the variable cost (mainly electricity for pumps, polymers and chlorine) by the average design volume.

All the components are updated based on the relevant national indexes that apply, such as the electricity index, chemicals index, salaries index and inflation.

5.2   Incentive clauses

Guiding principle: *Appropriate incentives to encourage successful performance (against carefully chosen indicators and targets that relate to the contract's objectives) should be included in the contract. Redundant incentives (success incentives that are not achievable) should be avoided.*

The use of incentive clauses, or payment terms that have incentive elements, are becoming increasingly common in service and management contracts. This is because incentives enable clients to motivate operators/contractors to perform better on those service aspects that the client considers important. If the incentive clauses are carefully selected and monitored, successful 'win-win' outcomes can be achieved, provided the operator is able to make the necessary improvements. In selecting suitable incentive clauses, the client should consider the aspects below.

a) The incentives should be based on measurable indicators and **targets that relate to the clients' own objectives** (which should be based on detailed studies of system performance). Example indicators could be increase in billing efficiency, increase in volume of water sold, reduced 'down time'—non operational time—for particular installations or a reduction in meter reading errors

b) **Accurate measurement and verification** of performance against the incentive clause indicator should be achievable by both the operator and the client's representative, in order to minimize disputes. Incentives such as increased billing efficiency or time to complete repairs usually meet this requirement. Choosing incentives based on easily measurable indicators is important.

c) **Incentives targets should be set that are realistically achievable** by an able operator during the course of a contract. So a balance needs to be struck—the incentive should be paid for good or excellent performance, but it should not reward mediocre or poor performance. Setting incentive targets that are too high can result in redundant incentives; such targets should be avoided as they create false expectations.

d) **Setting the incentive payment amounts** requires careful judgement. Payment should be large enough to encourage good operator performance, but not so large that it deprives the client of much needed revenues.

Box 5.3. Summary of incentive payments in a contract in Puebla, Mexico (1998)[1]

The services being managed by this management contract in Puebla, Mexico, include metering, database development, water billing, collection and customer services. Incentives are only provided for billing and collection, according to the following procedure.

The indicator is the collection efficiency (collection/billing), which is measured every six months. This is then compared with the previous period to measure the increase/decrease in efficiency. The efficiency gains provide an economic incentive as the operator is rewarded by a percentage increase to the service cost according to the following table:

Collection efficiency for the period in %	Additional payment as a % of service costs
0 - 40	0.0
40 - 50	0.2
50 - 60	0.4
60 - 70	0.7
70 - 80	1.4
80 - 90	2.3
90 - 100	3.5

The collection figures exclude late payments of previous period bills.

---

1. Source: Morale–Reyes, Sansom and Franceys, case study in Sansom et al, 2003 (Volume 2)

The examples of incentive clauses that are set out in Box 5.3, Box 5.4, Box 5.5 and Box 5.6 show the diversity of options available for such clauses, These examples are by no means exhaustive. Careful design of incentives to suit specific circumstance and context is required in order to ensure that they are fair to both parties and act as an effective motivation for improvements in operations.

The use of incentives related to improvements in bill collections has the advantage of being easily measurable provided the monitoring information is correctly managed and verified. Such clauses can also be used as incentives to improve O&M and customer services, where these aspects are included in the contract. This is because satisfied customers are more likely to pay their bills promptly.

Another type of incentive that can be used relates to the percentage of accurate water meter readings, or non-readings, of meters (refer to Box 5.5 for an example from Chile). Such incentives can work well where there is a comprehensive monitoring programme that verifies the readings based on careful checking of the operator's performance by the client's representative. In determining target levels, the client needs to be aware of the practicalities of the contract tasks so that it does not penalize the operators unfairly.

Box 5.4. Example of incentives—Pune draft billing and collection contract[1]

Although this contract did not proceed, many of the clauses were concisely written. For example, the incentive clause to this contract is set out below.

'The operator will be eligible for a premium for improved collections of water charges over and above the minimum annual collection targets that are specified by the employer. The premium shall be 10 per cent of the additional collections and shall be payable on an annual basis.'

Note: the client will need to ensure that it is not being too generous to the operator with a clause such as this, particularly where larger than expected tariff increases occurs during the contract period. In such a case the operator would receive larger incentive payments due to the tariff increase, without its having to do any additional work. For such clauses it is advisable to include the assumed tariff increases over the contract period in the contract.

---

1.   *Source: Pune Municipal Corporation draft contract, India (1998)*

Box 5.5. Example of incentives/penalties—EMOS meter reading contract[1]

EMOS, a water company in Chile, was concerned about the high percentage of non-reading of water meters on one of its contracts. In 1999, it introduced an incentives and penalties clause to reduce this problem. The main elements of the clause were as follows. Note that 3.8 per cent of meters not read is the accepted standard that would result in neither an incentive nor a penalty being paid:

Percentage range of meters not read	Incentive or penalty paid
3.6 - 3.8%	Two more readings paid (to operator)
3.0 - 3.6%	Three more readings paid (to operator)
If more than 3.8%	One reading payment deducted (penalty)

These incentives encouraged the meter readers to be resourceful, particularly in going to houses when the occupiers are likely to be at home. Another important incentive offered to employees was for detecting and reporting illegal connections or bypasses. The incentive payment was equivalent to 17 per cent of their basic salary.

---

1.   *Source: Morales-Reyes and Franceys, case study in Sansom et al, 2003 (Volume 2)*

For the larger contracts, such as the Johannesburg water management contract, a number of incentives can be used to encourage the operator to make the expected improvements across a range of activities (refer to Box 5.6 for a summary of the incentive provisions on this contract). Other examples of incentive clauses, such as the incentive formula for the disconnection and reconnection contract in Chile, are given in Volume 2 on case studies and contract analysis (Sansom et al, 2003).

5.3   Penalty clauses

Guiding principle: Appropriate penalties should be included in the contract to discourage poor performance against carefully chosen indicators and targets that relate to the contract's objectives.

Box 5.6. Johannesburg contract—remuneration and incentives[1]

The operators' remuneration consists of three components.

- A fixed management fee that is linked to service delivery.

- Incentive A (up to Rand 20 million) for human resource development, capital expenditure, program delivery, sewer overflow discharge results, customer services and O&M of facilities measured in terms of plant downtime.

- Incentive B is about profit sharing, it is a percentage of the improved operating margin.

---

1. *Source: A. Still, GJMC presentation, 2001*

Contract payments should preferably be linked to outputs in order to encourage service improvements or efficiencies. Good or excellent performance can be rewarded through incentive payments, while poor performance can be discouraged through appropriate penalty clauses. In selecting suitable penalty clauses, the client should consider the aspects below.

a) The penalty should be **based on measurable indicators and targets that relate to the clients' own objectives**. For example, unacceptably low bill collection efficiency, or a decrease in volume of water sold, or excessive 'down time'—non-operational time— for particular installations.

b) **Accurate measurement and verification of performance** against the penalty clause indicator should be achievable by both the operator and the client's representative, in order to minimize disputes. Financial penalties, such as those that relate to poor bill collection efficiency, usually meet this requirement. However, indicators such as 'unsatisfactory down time for particular installations,' may not always be appropriate if, for example, it is difficult to differentiate between non-operational times caused by power supply failures, or if down time is due to the operator's inability to carry out repairs promptly.

c) **Levels of performance that cause penalty clauses to come into effect** should not be set so the operator is penalized unfairly. The penalty clause should only apply if performance is poor or significantly below what is expected of a competent operator or contractor. Where there are legitimate reasons for the inadequate performance due to factors outside the operator's control, the client should consider each case on an impartial basis.

d) **Setting the penalty clause payment amounts** requires careful judgement. The payment should be large enough to discourage poor operator performance, but not so large that it deters bidders from taking on the risks.

Examples of penalty clauses are summarized in Box 5.7, Box 5.8 and Table 5.1, as well as in Box 5.5. For new contracts, specific penalty and incentive clauses need to be developed that are appropriate for each individual situation. In many cases the penalty and incentive clauses need to be developed and refined together so that an appropriate balance of 'carrot and stick' is provided. Examples of clauses where there is such a balance of penalties and incentives are shown in Box 5.5 and Box 5.6.

Box 5.7. Ajmer Pipelines contract: penalty and incentive clauses[1]

An O&M contract was let in 1995 in Rajasthan, India, for 112 km of transmission pipelines. The penalty and incentive clauses are summarized below. They have contributed to a reported reduction in the average time taken to repair burst pipes and leaks.

Penalty for delay in repairs beyond the specified period	
Period of delay beyond specified period	Penalty (Rupees/hour)
0 - 2 hours	500
2 - 4 hours	750
4 - 8 hours	1,000
Beyond 8 hours	2,500

Incentives clause

If the contractor completes the work earlier than the stipulated period, he or she shall be allowed an incentive payment as summarized below.

1. When 5% of the completion period is saved, he/she is entitled to an additional payment of 1% of the actual cost of work.

2. When 7.5% of the completion period is saved, he/she is entitled to an additional payment of 1.5% of the actual cost of work.

3. When 10% or more of the completion period is saved, he is entitled to an additional payment of 2% of the actual cost of work.

1.   Source: Govt of Rajasthan, PHED, Ajmer, Govt. of Rajasthan pipelines contract, India

Box 5.8. Summary of penalty provisions in a contract in Puebla, Mexico (1998)[1]

The services being managed as part of this management contract in Puebla, Mexico, include metering, database development, water billing, collection and customer services. Penalties can be charged in cases where the failure is due to the contractor, as summarized below.

- Due to delays on tasks: 20% base charge and a 30% additional charge if the task was finished after 1 to 3 month's delay, depending of the service type.

- If a failure by the contractor caused the collecting efficiencyto be reduced, the contractor pays 5% of the equivalent amount that was not collected.

- If a task is not completed, the contractor is fined 5% of the total amount.

- If the contractor refuses to undertake a specific contract annex as a whole, he/she pays 10% of the total corresponding value.

1.   *Source: Morales-Reyes, Sansom and Franceys, case study in Sansom et al 2003*

Table 5.1. Penalty clauses for Redhills water treatment plant, Chennai[1]

	Penalty
1. If the quantity of treated water is less than 90% of raw water supplied	10 rupees per 1,000 litres of shortfall
2. If the quality of treated water fails in any one of the prescribed parameters in a day	2,000 rupees per million litres
3. If the quantity of water used for washing the filter bed increases beyond 40 cubic metres per one MLD of treated water	0 rupees per 1,000 litres
4. If the key personnel are not employed as per the list	Rate at double the pay scale

1. Source: CMWSB contract, India, 1997

5.4   Specified payment process

Guiding principle: The payment process should be specified in the contract, including interim payments, the period within which payments should be made and adjustments for inflation (where necessary). There should be provision for delays in payments and methods of compensation (such as interest) for the delays, including interruption of work or termination of the contract.

A carefully specified payment procedure with adequate provision for delays, that is diligently followed by both parties, can contribute significantly to an effective working relationship. Such a payment procedure can also assist in reducing the risk of corruption as the operator will be less tempted to seek to bribe the client's employees in order to receive sums of money that are owed to it.

An example of a payment procedure in a draft contract from Pune, India, is shown in Box 5.9. This covers many of the important points.

5.5   Open book accounting

Guiding principle: Open-book accounting for contracted services is desirable as a means of improving transparency and is an aid to resolving disputes.

While not all service and management contracts require open book accounting, there are a number of advantages in making this accounting method a requirement in the contract, particularly for management contracts associated with service provision. One reason is that management contracts often have a weakness in that it is difficult to specify which type of repairs should be included in the management fee (so the risk is borne by the operator) and which type of repairs (particularly larger repairs) should be paid for separately by the client. By having comprehensive open book accounting, the client can allow specified large repair works to be paid for separately, but there will still be detailed accounts to enable checks for value for money.

Box 5.9. Example of a payment procedure - Pune contract[1]

This draft contract for billing and collection in Pune had the following payment procedure clause.

'For the lump sum payment, the operator shall submit an application for payment within 15 days of the due date for payment. For the management fees, the operator shall submit *with supporting documentation,* an application for payments within the first 15 days of each month in respect of the services provided since the last date covered by the previous payment and any other outstanding amounts.

'Supporting documentation shall include, without limitations, statements of:

a. progress achieved by the operator relating to (i) databases on properties and connections, ii) billing and collection systems, iii) policies on billing and collection and iv) customer services;

b. bank statements of bills for water charges, fines and reconnection fees collected by the operator;

c. calculations on any amount due or owing arising from incentives or penalty deductions;

d. calculations of interest on late payments due to or from the employer.

'The amount due to the operator under any payment certificate issued by the PMU (who monitors the contract), shall be paid to the operator within 28 days after such interim payment certificate has been issued. Only such portion of the application that is not adequately supported within the scope and definition of the contract may be withheld from payment.

'Should any discrepancy be found to exist between the actual payment and the correct amount due to the operator, the employer (client) may add or subtract the differences from any subsequent payments. In the event of the failure of the employer to make payment within the time stated, the employer shall pay to the operator interest at a rate equal to the current average bank rate.'

---

1. *Source: Pune Municipal Corporation, draft management contract, 1998*

Open book accounting should also provide valuable information to support the resolution of disputes.

Where open book accounting is a step too far, perhaps where there is limited capacity in the client's accounting department to make good use of the facility (though, of course, that activity could be contracted out), regular financial reporting should be a minimum requirement. An example clause is covered in Box 5.10.

5.6   Guarantees for the client

Guiding principle*: Appropriate guarantees for the client should be agreed and clearly specified in the contract.*

Clients typically seek to have financial provisions or guarantee in case they have to incur expense due to poor performance of the operator during the course of the contract. Often a figure of 5 or 10 per cent of the annual contract value is required in the form of a security deposit or bank guarantee. The client then has discretion to use this money in the case of default by the operator or contractor, in accordance with the contract.

Box 5.10. Ugandan small towns contracts—accounting[1]

Under the contract for the management of water services (including O&M, billing and collection) in small towns in Uganda, the following provision is included concerning the presentation of accurate accounts of the operator's transactions.

'The operator shall, in respect of each quarter of a financial year and no later than 30 days after the end of the quarter, prepare a report to the Authority containing:

a. information about, and an analysis of, its operations for the quarter and cumulatively for the year to date; and

b. financial statements in accordance with the prescribed manner and generally accepted principles for the quarter and cumulative for the year to date.

---

1. Source: The Republic of Uganda's standard management contract for small towns, 2001

Provisions are also usually made to cover the risk of the assets not being left in a serviceable condition by the operator at the end of a contract. To cover this risk, clients often have a retention or similar provision in the contract. This entails retaining a defined sum for typically a year after the contract ends to enable the client to finance any rectifications that are required as a result of any operator's neglect.

5.7 Guarantees for the operator

Guiding principle: Appropriate guarantees for the contractor/operator should be agreed and clearly specified in the contract.

Operators considering bidding for a contract will typically be seeking written guarantees in the contract on a number of aspects. First, they will seek written assurances that their interim payment claims will be paid on time and that if there are any delays they will be paid a fair rate of interest for the duration of the delay. A typical clause covering these aspects is shown in Box 5.9 on the payment procedure on a draft contract from Pune in India.

The operator will also likely to seek guarantees that any dispute resolution will be conducted impartially with adjudication procedures that should be specified in the contract. Assurances that the client will arrange for the granting of approvals, such as access to land and other necessary government approvals, should also be stipulated in the contract, under the 'obligations of the employer or client' section. In essence, the more written reassurances that the client can give to potential bidders that they will be treated fairly, the better and, potentially, the lower the bid will be.

Chapter 6

Partnership aspects

6.1   Defining roles and duties

Guiding principle: The contract documents should clearly define roles and duties of all involved. The   organization system for the implementation of the contract should be specified. There should be separation of the roles of Contract Administrator (representing the client), Project Manager (representing the operator) and an independent adjudicator.

By clearly specifying the roles, duties and obligations of all parties in the contract, there is much less scope for confusion and dispute during the implementation of the contract. Box 6.1 shows the main clause headings and responsibilities for a management contract in Uganda.

6.2   Developing win-win situations

Guiding principles: The contract documents should reflect a specific duty requiring both parties to deal fairly with each other with shared financial motivation and a general presumption to achieve 'win-win' solutions to problems that may arise during the course of the contract.

When using traditional forms of contract, adversarial approaches often develop between the client's representative and the operator or contractor, as part of a 'claims culture.' Consequently, a lot of time is devoted to resolving the disputes that arise from the adversarial situation. An alternative, better way of working is to seek to deal fairly with both parties and pursue 'win-win' solutions to problems that may arise.

A good starting point is for the client and its representatives to understand the typical perspectives and motivating factors for private contractors or operators. Contractors exist to meet various business objectives, just as utility organizations exist to meet their own objectives. To regard contractors as purely profit maximization organizations is an over-simplification (Broome, 1999). Contractors usually have three broad objectives that are relevant here.

1.   In the short term, contractors aim to make a positive cash flow to pay their bills. This is because if the expenditure exceeds income over a sustained period of time, then

---

Box 6.1. Ugandan small towns contracts—roles and duties[1]

Under the contract for the management of water services (including O&M, billing and collection) in small towns in Uganda, details of the obligations of the operator and authority (client/employer) are given under the following headings:

Obligations and duties of the operator

- To safeguard, use, manage and control assets

- To provide operation and maintenance services

- To manage non-routine and urgent repairs and minor extensions to the system

- To charge and collect for services provided

- To receive a management fee

- To maintain and keep records

- To prepare and submit business plans

- To report to the authority or employer (covering aspects such as financial statements and performance on all contract activities) in the prescribed manner

- To allow inspections

- To be indemnified against all claims (provided the operator uses due diligence and care)

Obligations and duties of the authority (employer)

- To set tariffs, rates and charges

- To pay a management fee

- To audit accounts

- Not to interfere with operations.

---

1. *Source: The Republic of Uganda's standard management contract for small towns, 2001*

a company will not be able to continue operating. In general, the more positive cash flow there is, the more profit a company makes, either through not paying interest or through being paid interest. Delay in payment can have serious effects on profit margin and a huge effect on return on investment.

2. Contractors wish to produce a profit on any contract they enter into. They prefer profit levels from a contract to be predictable rather than fluctuating and unpredictable. For any firm or business, not knowing when or how much it will be paid for completed work does not aid the running of that business. It is therefore important for the contractor to know when and how much payment will be forthcoming.

3. Contractors generally want a satisfied employer, so that they can win repeat orders or referred business. The 'generally' depends on the employer. For instance, if the next contract will be awarded on the basis of lowest cost criteria whatever the contractor's performance on the previous contract, or if the employer is unlikely to place another contract, then the aim of a satisfied employer may be subjugated in order to pursue the first two objectives.

If the employer or client seeks to deal fairly with the operator/contractor and pursue win-win opportunities, then it will in effect be encouraging the operator to focus on objective 3) listed above. As a result the client will be working towards enhancing its reputation and providing good services, to the mutual benefit of both parties.

Experience shows that successful contracts are those that are conducted on the basis of mutual trust because, although detailed specifications and monitoring are necessary, it is difficult to make such contracts entirely comprehensive. It is important to be sure that the contractor is reasonably comfortable with his/her obligations and that the specified payment is reasonable. If the contractor's margins are too tight (UK Government, 1986), the following implications are likely:

• he/she will employ insufficient staff;

• he/she will pay too little, and therefore employ unsuitable staff;

• either way, the standard of service will decline;

• he/she will not have the resources to respond to complaints;

• he/she will skimp on liaison with the client, making it more difficult to get things put right; and

• he/she may cut corners on health and safety, with potentially damaging repercussions for the client.

None of these outcomes are desirable, hence the need to include flexible payment mechanisms that reward good performance. Pursuing win-win outcomes requires a holistic approach both in contract development and management, addressing the issues raised in the guiding principles in this document.

6.3   Autonomy for the operator's personnel

Guiding principle: The contractor should have autonomy over its own personnel, although minimum requirements for key staff may be stated (such as minimum qualifications and experience).

Where water supply organizations who have been managing services decide to contract out all or part of those services, the client water supply organization can tend to 'interfere' unnecessarily in the work of the operator. For private companies to achieve efficiency gains or service improvements, they need the freedom to innovate and make changes, perhaps using new methods or technologies.

If a good performance-based contract is prepared, than the client representatives can concentrate on checking that the operator is meeting its agreed performance requirements, rather than becoming too involved in the day-to-day management of services. Box 6.2 includes an example of a clause in a Ugandan management contract that is designed to minimize unnecessary interference in the operator's work.

6.4   Dispute resolution

Guiding principle: A speedy method of dispute resolution should be clearly set out in the contract documents and an impartial adjudicator acceptable to both parties specified.

Box 6.2. Example clause—'not to interfere with operations'[1]

A management contract used for water service provision in selected small towns in Uganda contains the following clause to encourage the local municipality to deal fairly with the operator.

'The provisions in this contract not withstanding, the authority (*client*) shall not interfere with the day-to-day operations of the operator. In particular, the authority shall not:

a. issue instructions to the operator regarding operational decisions or actions, except by way of the authority's approved business plan in accordance with the provisions of the performance contract or by way of a schedule issued under clause 18 (*concerning tariffs and charges);*

b. issue instructions to an operator or attempt to influence an operator's decision regarding the connection of a customer to the water supply system, or regarding a disconnection made by the operator or any lawful action taken by the operator regarding non-payment by a customer;

c. withhold payments due to the operator on account of the operator refusing or failing to comply with instructions issued in contravention of this clause; and

d. contravention of this clause by the authority shall constitute a breach of this contract subject to termination of the contract under clause 24.

---

1. *Source: Republic of Uganda's standard management contract for small towns, 2001*

In the event of a dispute between the parties to the contract, it is better to attempt to negotiate a solution that is fair and reasonable to both parties before resorting to arbitration. Box 6.3 shows an 'amicable settlement' clause from a draft contract in Pune, India, which has been included in order to encourage such a co-operative approach between the signatories to the contract.

Box 6.3. Amicable settlement clause—Pune draft management contract[1]

'The parties hereto agree to use reasonable efforts to resolve any disagreements or disputes concerning the interpretation or implementation of this contract through mutual consultation and negotiation. The project steering committee shall act as a 'dispute resolution committee' for this purpose. The contracting parties share the desire and intention of co-operating in a good and trusting climate within the framework of the provisions of this contract...'

---

1. *Source: Pune Municipal Corporation, draft management contract, 1998*

If in the event that both parties are unable to resolve a particular dispute after careful negotiations, then an impartial arbitration process should be available to either party. Box 6.4 shows an example of an arbitration clause from a Ugandan contract (note that the clause allows for a mutually agreeable arbitrator and for the arbitration process being conducted in accordance with a government act).

In a contract for the operation and maintenance of the wastewater treatment plant in the city of Torreon, in Mexico, a sequential process of disagreements and dispute resolutions is included, which is summarized in Box 6.5. The main objectives of such a clause are to encourage a partnership approach, to minimize protracted disputes and to reduce the number of times it is necessary to go to the law courts.

Box 6.4. Ugandan small towns contracts—arbitration clause[1]

'Any dispute arising between parties in connection with this contract shall be submitted to an arbitrator to be appointed by agreement between the parties or, failing such agreement, by the Director, within 30 days after one party first serves notice on the other of such dispute. Any such arbitration proceedings shall be conducted in accordance with and subject to the provisions of the Arbitration Act (Chapter 49).'

---

1. *Source: Republic of Uganda's standard management contract for small towns, 2001*

Box 6.5. Torrean sequential dispute resolution clause, Mexico[1]

a. If a disagreement arises, initially the parties will negotiate and try to solve the matters of dispute in a partnership environment, considering the contract agreement and seeking the best solution for the project objectives.

   (A maximum period is stated to solve the issue)

b. If the negotiations continue and the dispute cannot be solved by dialogue, the contract committee that monitors the contract will be called to discuss the dispute and to seek the best solution. If agreed, the committee will ask a third party for its opinion on the dispute. After further discussion, the committee may agree to accept the third party's opinion as a final resolution.

   (Both parties share the third party's costs)

c. The third option is dispute arbitration through the National Centre for Arbitration. In this case, should the parties accept the resolution, the loser pays the costs involved.

d. The final option is court procedures as stated in the law.

---

1. *(Source: Morales-Reyes, 2003)*

For contracts that involve international companies, international arbitration rules should be considered, such as the International Centre for Settlements of Investment of disputes (ICSID), the International Federation of Consulting Engineers or the International Chamber of Commerce.

6.5   Specified method of financing and procedures

Guiding principle: The method of financing the contract should be clearly specified.

It is worthwhile specifying how the contract will be financed, whether from water charges or from government funds, or both. A separate account could be maintained by the client to ensure that money is always available to pay the operator promptly. It is also important for the client to clarify the financial decision making procedures and processes in the contract. This will enable potential bidders to feel more confident about being reimbursed on time. The inclusion of other clauses, covering aspects such as provisions for late payment and impartial dispute adjudication, should have the collective effect of developing improved levels of trust between the operator and client.

6.6 Monitoring and evaluation

Guiding principle: Provisions for the client's monitoring and evaluation should be included in the contract.

The monitoring and evaluation requirements should be clearly specified in the contract provisions. The particular performance requirements, payment terms, penalty and incentive clauses give the main indicators that the operator's performance should be measured against.

Close monitoring by the client's representative is required in order to determine the correct payments against unit rate items and penalty or incentive clauses. For example, if payment is dependent on 'the percentage of correct meter readings,' then systematic monitoring systems are required to verify performance levels in this area. When measuring operator performance on a sampling basis, the margins of sampling error will need to be defined.

Typical provisions in the contract for adequate monitoring and evaluation could include the aspects below.

- **The operator is to keep records** in the prescribed manner, covering all the key aspects of service provision and the financial aspects.

- **The operator is to allow adequate inspection** by the client's representatives at any time, including viewing all assets, services provided and records kept, permitting copies of records and photographs to be taken where necessary.

- **The operator is to allow any tests** to be undertaken.

- **The operator is to submit reports** in the prescribed manner on a regular basis (e.g. quarterly), to attend meetings and make presentations, as required.

- **The operator is to carry out any of the client's instructions** (which are in accordance with the contract) that arise from the ongoing monitoring, or to seek to resolve any dispute in the prescribed manner.

The monitoring or regulatory authority will also want to follow up on any complaints received about the service provided or the performance of the operator, as well as to survey citizen or user satisfaction wherever possible. The client's representative will also need to report any findings from site inspections or analyses of reports, both to the client and the operator.

It is important to establish clear channels of communication between the main contract stakeholders at the outset. If the main parties to the contract deal with each other firmly but fairly, then win-win outcomes for all stakeholders are more likely to occur.

6.7 Management attributes for effective contracting out

Whether small service contracts are let for activities such as meter reading, or larger management contracts are developed for O&M, billing and customer services, the contract(s) should ideally be part of a wider reform or change programme at the utility/

municipality. Indeed, contracting out can make an effective contribution to reform by encouraging competition, efficiency and output-based approaches.

Senior managers who are overseeing contract development should preferably have knowledge, skills and experience of effective utility management and commercial approaches. Section 7.2 outlines some of the typical commercial approach measures that can be introduced. Where utility managers do not have the required knowledge and skills, or they do not have sufficient time, capable consultants can be appointed to provide guidance on the contract development and management process.

Amongst the utility or host organization team who are managing the development, monitoring, enforcement and evaluation of the contract, the typical indicative attributes are as below, using the ASKE (Attitudes, Skills, Knowledge and Experience) framework.

Attitudes

- A commitment to continuous improvement
- A willingness to adopt more commercial approaches
- A willingness to seek win-win situations and deal fairly with both parties
- A willingness to learn from experiences elsewhere
- A willingness to work productively with people from other disciplines and organizations

Skills

- Good communication and listening skills
- Negotiation skills
- Analytical and report writing skills
- Ability to think broadly linking technical, financial, social and institutional issues

Knowledge of:

- Output-based contracts with incentives and penalties
- The specific objectives and context of the contract
- Broader utilities management and commercial approaches
- Systems development

Experience of:

- The services being contracted out
- Contract management
- Strategic, tactical and operational planning

For different contract arrangements, such as smaller contracts, some of the suggested attributes listed above may be merely desirable, rather than essential. It should also be remembered that the best way of learning is by doing. Utilities should not be deterred from contracting out if they do not have all the required ASKE attributes. It is better to contract out using smaller contracts so that lessons can be learnt and later contract development and management can be improved.

Where there is a need to strengthen in-house capacity in contract development and management, suitable human resource development (HRD) initiatives can be developed by the utility and linked to broader HRD programmes within that organization.

6.8   Contingency planning

Utilities or municipalities should anticipate the consequences of total or partial contract failure. If a contract is well prepared, let and well managed, the likelihood of a contractor withdrawing should be limited. However, if termination of a contract does take place, or a contractor voluntarily withdraws, utilities should have contingency plans. Utilities should analyse the likely effects of failure to identify what the core aspects of the service are, and how they could provide those activities at short notice. For each activity, utilities should determine what they would need to do immediately after failure—in the first week, the first month, and the first six months until the contract can be re-let.

Contingency planning should include financial considerations. Where contracts are paid in arrears, money will be available to cover additional costs incurred by the termination of the contract. Further costs may be claimed from the contractor, depending on the arbitration and termination terms of the contract. Utilities mainly use performance bonds and sometimes parent company guarantees. Such bonds or guarantees require private contractors to make arrangements with a financial institution so that, should the contract fail, funding will be available to provide the service, at least in the short term. In effect, contractors have to arrange for insurance cover by paying a premium to the financial institution.

Performance bonds do have disadvantages in that the insurance company or bank may delay payment or contest the claim and this may lead to lengthy legal arguments. Another disadvantage of performance bonds is that they effectively limit the number of tenderers, since smaller companies may be unable to provide performance bonds. The advantage of performance bonds is that they serve as a reference to a potential contractor's creditworthiness (that is, the bank or insurance company is prepared to underwrite the contractor).

Experience shows that none of the parties to a contract benefit from contract failure (apart from lawyers engaged by both parties). It is therefore recommended that a utility should concentrate on minimizing the likelihood of contractor failure by getting the other elements of the client role right and by building a collaborative relationship with the contractor. This is especially so for contracts involving infrastructure projects such as water and sanitation services that are typically viewed as essential services.

Chapter 7

Developing an enabling environment

7.1   Enabling legislation and policies

If private sector participation is to be developed on a substantial basis, it will be necessary for a government to develop an enabling environment at city, state and national level, addressing key constraints. The policy areas and legislation below should be examined to ensure that they do not adversely effect the contracting out of services:

a) Employment law and conditions of service

b) General legislation allowing or permitting private sector involvement

c) Policies and practice concerning decentralisation and distribution of organization responsibilities

d) Water laws and water resources management

e) Tax liability

f) Contract law

g) Competition and procurement rules

h) Health and safety regulations

i) Social polices (e.g. disconnection rights and subsidies)

j) Government funding, risk management and guarantees

k) Standard forms of contract and regulatory arrangements.

It is generally more important for governments to examine these matters in detail when public utilities are contemplating larger contracts. More detailed guidance on enabling legislation and policies is provided by the World Bank publication *Toolkits for Private Participation in Water and Sanitation*, 1997.

7.2   Commercial approaches

A key lesson that emerges from the contracting out case studies and contract analyses is that where there is an effective commercial orientation in the water utility as well as in the contractor/operator, there is a greater chance of successful contract outcomes. Effective commercial and customer orientation implies that a number of aspects are addressed, either within or outside the contract.

Potential measures for the urban water sector that can deliver improvements are likely to include many of the following, under the three main headings of commercial systems development, human resources management and policy and organizational development. Many utilities will have already undertaken a lot of these measures, while others still have much to do.

7.2.1 Commercial systems development

a) **Creating separate water and sewerage budgets** and balancing expenditure with income each month so that funds are always available for programmed and emergency work. This improves the water sector managers' ability to manage resources.

b) **Instituting commercial accounting for water and sewerage services** in order to generate useful management information, such as financial ratios, that are invaluable in determining the priorities for improvement.

c) **Introducing separate water bills (including sewerage charges)** rather than combining water charges in the general council bills. This improves accountability, as tariff increases can be linked to service improvements in the minds of the customers.

d) **Using performance indicators and benchmarking effectively.** Such indicators could include: average water consumption per household in each area; average supply hours in each area; unaccounted for water (UFW); percentage of residents served directly in each area; number of breakdowns; and number of complaints. Reliable information against such indicators enables a water utility to assess its performance and set realistic targets for improvement.

e) **Introducing asset management systems—maximizing the life and effectiveness of assets** through maintaining up-to-date records of the location, condition and performance of those assets (such as water treatment plants, pipelines and pumping equipment). Undertaking preventative maintenance and replacing those assets that are either in poor condition or are performing inadequately.

f) **Setting water and sewerage tariffs at sustainable levels** so as to generate sufficient funds to maintain the assets and services, to pay all debt charges, as well as to expand infrastructure and services to unserved areas, in a sustainable manner.

g) **Improving customer services** by measures such as:

- introducing local customer service offices;

- having a single window system for dealing with all customer requests and problems;

- introducing a customer charter;

- streamlining procedures for new connections and paying bills;

- maintaining an up-to-date customer database after detailed surveys of all connections;

- introducing call centres for complaints and requests, linked to effective complaint redressal systems;

- developing a customer consultative committee that is representative of all areas of the city; and

- reducing unauthorized water and sewerage connections by measures such as temporary amnesties for regularizing connections.

h) **Developing comprehensive O&M management systems** based on preventative maintenance and prompt completion of repairs.

i) **Reducing unaccounted for water** through measures such as leak detection programmes, bulk metering and individual meters for each customer.

j) **Introducing computerized billing systems** linked to the financial management, meter reading and other systems.

k) **Using the private sector effectively and efficiently** to provide discreet inputs (e.g. service contracts) or broader management of services (e.g. management contracts), or more complex PPP arrangements such as lease and concession contracts, where appropriate.

l) **Improving contract management systems** for procuring consultancy services and supplies.

7.2.2 Human resources management

a) **Introducing management development programmes** for senior and middle level staff, to improve their management of staff and enable them to adopt effective water utility management practices.

b) **Developing and implementing comprehensive training plans for all staff**, based on detailed training needs analyses and developing attitudes, skills, knowledge and experience (ASKE), building on the evaluation of the training.

c) **Seeking partnerships with appropriate training institutions** so that well designed, customized capacity building programmes can be developed, based on agreed organizational objectives.

d) **Attracting and retaining staff with the required skills** to meet the organizational objectives, and providing adequate remuneration, recruiting from the open market where necessary.

e) **Increasing delegation of duties and staff authority limits**, allied to new objective-orientated job descriptions, and redeploying staff where necessary.

f) **Implementing open staff appraisals** using agreed formats and linking this process to organizational objectives and the forthcoming training programme.

g) **Increasing the status of key posts,** such as managers dealing with O&M, customer services, financial management and services to poor areas.

h) **Reducing of the number of staff per thousand connections** in order to reduce costs and develop a proactive attitude to work.

i) **Developing staff incentives,** including measures such as promotion on merit and bonus schemes.

j) **Introducing pilot change initiatives** to bring about organizational improvements, encouraging teams from different departments to work together.

k) **Implementing induction programmes** for new staff to encourage them to work effectively towards organizational objectives.

7.2.3   Policy and organizational development

a) **Agreeing specific objectives, strategic plans and policies** for urban water and sewerage services over the coming 10 to 20 years, based on a detailed assessment of the current service levels and problems.

b) **Completing the decentralization of responsibilities** from state/central government and agencies to municipal corporations or utilities.

c) **Improving the autonomy of the 'service provider'** for water and sewerage services, including integration of aspects such as O&M, billing, financial management, customer services etc. within the same department or agency.

d) **Undertaking organizational restructuring** in order to meet the utility's objectives, giving more emphasis to key functions such as O&M, customer services, billing, services for the poor and financial management, while maintaining the co-operation of staff and other stakeholders.

e) **Establishing clear 'service provider' and 'enabling agency' or regulator** roles for specific organizations and providing support and resources to enable them to fulfil those roles.

f) **Enabling legislation for Public Private Partnerships** so that municipalities/utilities are able to contract out the management of water and sewerage services, including services for customers, if they so wish.

g) **Developing new performance agreements** between service providers and enabling agencies, where agreed tariff increases are related to investment programmes and service improvements.

To achieve such reforms, both politicians and senior government officials will need to support the changes and be willing to transfer selected powers to the water authority managers and board members.

7.3   Regulation

The key issues related to regulation that need to be addressed include the following:

a) setting projected water and sewerage tariff levels;

b) ensuring responsiveness to customer needs;

c) ensuring price control, trading practices and value for money;

d) monitoring service standards and performance;ensuring asset serviceability over time;

e) ensuring water availability and use;

f) providing safety net regulations for the poor;

g) ensuring environmental and health standards;

h) promoting operating efficiency and water use efficiency; and

i) developing essential infrastructure.

These are the main responsibilities that remain with the government or regulator, regardless of which type of contract is used. Service and management contracts are relatively simple to regulate compared with the more complex lease, BOT and concession contracts. This is essentially because of their shorter duration and flexibility.

One of the most complicated regulation issues is setting projected tariff levels listed in (a) above, although this has less of an effect on service and management contracts compared with the more complex contracts. This is because payment on such contracts is normally based on unit prices or management fees, which are not dependent on tariffs. Care must be taken, however, where penalty or incentive clauses are related to revenue collected, which is of course related to tariff levels. Provided the organization letting the contract is transparent about proposed future tariff increases during the contract period, disputes should be minimized.

The decision concerning who should undertake the monitoring and regulation of the contract will depend on the size and scale of the contract. For service contracts with limited scope, the relevant department in the water utility or municipality can normally deal with the contract management/regulation, after having received appropriate training.

For larger management contracts, if there are doubts about the capacity of the local public sector to monitor and regulate a contract, reputable consultants can oversee regulation, as happened in Gaza for a water sector management contract. However, in most circumstances the water utility can regulate the management contract, as was the case in Johannesburg for the contract that was let in 2001. More detailed information that is relevant for larger contracts is included in the World Bank's *Toolkits for Private Participation in Water and Sanitation*, 1997.

7.4 Contractor development

For small and medium sized service/management contracts in developing countries, it is likely that, because of the size of the contracts, local companies will be the interested bidders,. The challenge is to encourage local companies to develop into effective and competitive operators.

For larger management contracts, international companies are likely to be interested, provided that they perceive the potential risks to be manageable and the enabling environment to be right. International operators and consultants, perhaps in conjunction with donor organizations, can also be a valuable resource in providing advice on sector reform and paving the way for effective public-private partnerships.

In terms of developing the capacity of the local private sector so that it will provide effective operators for water and sanitation services, there are a number of strategies that should be considered.

a) Involve both local and international companies in the sector reform process through workshops, study tours and preparation of consultancy reports.

b) Encourage international and local companies to form consortia, particularly for larger contracts.

c) Encourage public sector managers and staff to bid for new contracts. This was successfully done in Chile, where a number of water sector service contracts were let.

d) Provide informal and formal briefings to both public sector staff and capable local private companies, so as to encourage them to form companies to bid for forthcoming contracts. This approach was used in Uganda to encourage more local bids for small town water services management contracts.

e) Provide clear and comprehensive tender documents that will assist each bidder in understanding precisely what the client is seeking in terms of the bidding process, and in the technical and financial proposals it must submit.

Once the local private sector sees a potential market in the provision of water and sanitation services, it is likely to be more proactive in the water sector. This can contribute to its development, provided other aspects of the enabling environment are addressed.

7.5   Transfer or redeployment of staff

For smaller service-type contracts, staff transfer and redeployment tends to be less of a problem, as staff can generally be redeployed within the host organization or—by mutual agreement—the new operator can take on selected staff from the host utility. In Chile, for example, staff from the main utility were encouraged to set up their own companies to bid for service contracts, which worked reasonably well.

These issues tend to be more of a problem for larger contracts, such as management, lease and concession contracts, where redeployment of large numbers of staff within the host organization is not feasible. For shorter duration management contracts of 3 to 5 years, staff may be particularly concerned about their future employment and may request some form of official reassurance. There are a number of key transfer/redeployment issues to consider.

• Which staff can be redeployed within the host organization, with necessary retraining, and which staff can be retired?

• Which staff will be transferred to the new operator/contractor and what arrangements can be agreed for the protection of their conditions of employment?

• What is the process for determining if any redundancies are required and who should be made redundant, where necessary?

• What should be included in any voluntary redundancy packages?

• What should be the process for negotiations with key stakeholders, for example, with staff representatives such as unions and the preferred bidder?

• What arrangements (if any) should be agreed for transfer of staff working with the private operator at the end of the contract? Will they be transferred back to the host organization or another operator?

Many of these issues can be resolved through careful negotiations with the key stakeholders, who must all show a degree of flexibility. Where there are considerable difficulties in reaching agreement, potential strategies include employment protection legislation and Voluntary Competitive Tendering.

a) The introduction of employment protection legislation can provide a useful and consistent framework for resolving these complex issues. In the UK the 'Transfer of Undertakings (Protection of Employment) Regulations' (TUPE) were introduced in

1981. Further details on this legislation can be found at http://www.tssa.org.uk/advice/emp/emp20.htm

b) Voluntary Competitive Tendering (VCT) may be a more acceptable alternative for some stakeholders than direct contracting out. This is because in-house labour organizations can compete and win work against private sector organizations. Where this has been tried in the UK, in-house organizations still won a substantial proportion of the contracts let. The advantage of VCT is that it still provides incentives for efficiency gains and service improvements, but is often more acceptable to existing work forces. Further details are included in section 3.2.2.

7.6 Dissemination of lessons and further research

Whilst contracting out of water and sanitation services is increasing around the world, there are still many regions where it is a relatively new concept. It is therefore important that experiences in the use of service and management contracts be documented and disseminated, both to local audiences and to interested organizations in other countries.

Summarized below are key areas where further research and dissemination of lessons learnt in the use of service/management contracts (for water and sanitation services) is required.

a) Overall contract design, to encourage win-win outcomes and allocate risks to the parties best able to bear them.

b) The use of penalty and incentive clauses for different services that effectively encourage and reward good performance, without being too generous to the operator.

c) Appropriate payment terms for the management of routine maintenance work, as well as for urgent repairs and capital works programmes.

d) Effective and streamlined contract monitoring and regulation that encourages satisfactory performance without interfering too much in the day-to-day operations of the operator.

e) Best practice for dealing with existing workforces and the related problems of redundancy or re-deployment when contracting out services.

f) The transaction costs of designing, overseeing and enforcing contracts and preventing corruption require further research, particularly for well designed, output-based service and management contracts in the water sector. It should be noted that the transaction costs are significantly less for these types of contracts than for the more complex lease and concession contracts.

By continuing to share the important lessons from the use of such contracts, the benefits of contracting out services can be expected to increase. This will, in turn, contribute to the broader sector reform with subsequent improvements in service provision to consumers.

References

Andrisani, P. and S. Hakim (2000) *Making Government Work: Lessons Learned from America's Governors and Mayors*. Rowan & Littlefield: New York, USA.

Andersen Consulting (1993) 'Study on Outsourcing,' in M. Johnson *Outsourcing in brief*. Butterworth Heinemann: Oxford, UK.

Audit Commission, London (1993) *Realising the Benefits of Competition: The client role for contracted services*. HMSO: London, UK.

Bendor-Samuel, P. (undated) Frequently asked questions. *Outsourcing Journal*, http://www.outsourcing-faq.com/html/2.html

Brocklehurst C., and B. Evans (2001) *Serving Poor Consumers in South Asian Cities*. The Water and Sanitation Program-South Asia: India.

Blokland, M., O. Braadbaar and K. Schwartz (ed.) (1999) *Private Business, Public Owners. Government Shareholdings in Water Companies*. VROM: The Hague, the Netherlands.

Broome, Jon (1999) *The NEC Engineering and Construction Contract: A user's guide*. Thomas Telford Ltd: London, UK.

Chennai Metropolitan Water and Sewerage Board (1997) 'Management contract for Redhills water treatment plant.' Chennai, India.

CIPFA (1998) *A guide to Voluntary Competitive Tendering and Market Testing by Public Authorities.*, Competition Joint Committee: London, UK.

DETR (1999) *Implementing Best Value—A Consultation Paper on Draft Guidance*. Department for the Environment, Transport and the Regions: London, UK.

DFID (1998) *Improving Water Services through Competition*, DFID Occasional Paper No. 6. London Economics for DFID: London, UK.

EMOS (1998) Annual Report. Empresa Metropolitana de Obras Sanitarias S.A.: Santiago, Chile.

The Economist (1994) Farming out the farm. *The Economist* 5 March

The Economist (2000) Survey of the new economy, Don't do it yourself. *The Economist* 23 September 2000.

Finagua, S.C. (2001) 'Contracting and Finance for Water and Reuse.' Internal document. Mexico.

Government of Rajasthan, PHED (1996) *Tender documents for O&M of pipelines, pump houses and water treatment plants*. India. (unpublished)

Institution of Civil Engineers (1995) 'Professional Services Contract;' 2nd Edition, NEC document. Thomas Telford Services Ltd: London, UK.

Institution of Civil Engineers (1994) 'Professional Services Contract; Guidance notes;' 1st Edition. Thomas Telford Services Ltd: London, 1994.

Johnson, M. (1997) *Outsourcing in brief.* Butterworth Heinemann: Oxford, UK.

Keefer, Philip (1998) *Contracting out: an opportunity for public sector reform and private sector development in transition economies*. Finance and Private Sector Development, The World Bank: Washington D.C., USA.

KPMG (1995) *Impact Programme Outsourcing Working Group: Best practice guidelines for outsourcing.* HMSO: London, UK.

Latham M. (1994) *Constructing the team (principles for developing a modern contract).* Report on the construction industry in the UK. HMSO: London, UK.

Lorentzen J. (1998) *Overview of Issues and Strategic Options in Operations and Maintenance, Analysis and Synthesis Report (draft)*. UNCHS/Habitat Support Program for Urban Management: Nairobi, Kenya.

Morales-Reyes, J.I. (2004, forthcoming) 'Management and Services Contracts in the Mexican Water Sector.' PhD thesis, WEDC, Loughborough University, UK.

Oates, D, (1998) *Outsourcing and the Virtual Organization*. Century Business: London, UK.

Outsourcing Journal (2001) Accessed through outsourcing-journal.com, 2001.

Outsourcing Institute (1998) White Paper, written in association with Brown, Raysman, Millstein, Felder and Steiner. Outsourcing Institute:

Outsourcing Institute (1998) *Survey of Current and Potential Outsourcing End-Users*. The Outsourcing Institute:

Pune Municipal Corporation (1998) 'Draft billing and collection contract.' Maharashtra, India.

Republic of Uganda (2001) 'Standard Management contract for Small Towns used for Lyantonde town.' Uganda.

Safege consulting engineers, London Economics, Lyonaise des Eaux (now Ondeo) (1993) 'Draft interim report and management contract for water and sanitation. Bulgaria.

Sansom K.R., R.W.A.F. Franceys, J. Morales-Reyes and C. Njiru (2003) *Contracting out water and sanitation services, Volume 2—case studies and analysis of service and management contracts in developing countries.* WEDC: Loughborough University, UK.

Still, A. (2001) *The challenges of managing water and sanitation services in an African City.* A presentation made at the 2nd Regional conference on reform of the water and sanitation sector in Africa, Kampala, 26–28 February 2001.

UK Government (1986) *Using Private Enterprise in Government: Report of a multi-departmental review of competitive tendering and contracting for services in government departments.* HMSO: London, UK.

Witheford, David K. (1997) *Outsourcing of State Highway Facilities and Services.* National Cooperative Highway Research Program, National Academy Press: Washington D.C., USA

Walsh K., (1995) *Public Services and Market Mechanisms.* Macmillan: London, UK.

Water and Sanitation Program (WSP) and PPIAF (2002) *New Designs for Water and Sanitation Transactions—Making Private Sector Participation Work for the Poor.* WSP: Washington D.C., USA.

World Bank (1997) *Toolkits for Private Participation in Water and Sanitation.* World Bank: Washington D.C., USA

Glossary

ASKE	Attitudes, Skills, Knowledge and Experience
BOOT	Build, Own, Operate, Transfer
BOT	Build, Operate and Transfer
CBO	Community-Based Organization
CCT	Compulsory Competitive Tendering
CIPFA	Chartered Institute of Public Finance and Accountancy
CMWSB	Chennai Metro Water and Sewerage Board (India)
DBFO	Design, Build, Finance and Operate
DFID	Department For International Development (UK)
EMOS	Empresa Metropolitana de Obras Sanitarias S.A. (Chile)
GJMC	Greater Johannesburg Metropolitan Corporation
KRIP	Kampala Revenue Improvement Programme (Uganda)
MJP	Maharashtra Jeevan Pradhikaran (State Water Supply Agency, India)
MLD	Million Litres (of water) per Day
MLIC	Middle- and Low-Income Countries
NGO	Non-Governmental Organization
O&M	Operation and Maintenance
PHED	Public Health Engineering Department, India
PMU	Project Management Unit
PPP	Public Private Partnerships
PSP	Private Sector Participation
RFP	Request for Proposal
SESPA	Supplier Evaluation, Selection and Performance Appraisal
SSIP	Small-Scale Independent Providers
STWI	Severn Trent Water International
UFW	Unaccounted For Water
VCT	Voluntary Competitive Tendering

W&S   Water and Sanitation

WATSAN   Water and Sanitation

WSP-SA   Water and Sanitation Program—South Asia (World Bank)

www.ingramcontent.com/pod-product-compliance
Lightning Source LLC
Chambersburg PA
CBHW060957030426
42334CB00032B/3273